SOCIAL MEDIA

Secret Sauce

ADAM HOULAHAN

GW00697044

Published by Stenica Pty Ltd 2014

Copyright © 2014 Adam Houlahan

First Edition 2014

All rights reserved. No part of this publication may be reproduced, stored
in a retrieval system, or transmitted in any form or by any means, electronic,
mechanical, photocopying, recording or otherwise, without the prior written
permission from the publisher.

A catalogue record for this book is available from the National Library of Australia.

Book cover design and formatting services by BookCoverCafe.com

www.AdamHoulahan.com

ISBN: 978-0-9924698-0-1 (pbk)   978-0-9924698-1-8 (e-bk)

CONTENTS

FOREWORD

Thank you for purchasing a copy of *Social Media Secret Sauce*. It's great to know we'll be 'connecting' through all the insights I'm about to share with you.

In *Social Media Secret Sauce* I've shared my best knowledge on how you can grow your follower base in a truly cost-effective way. I've spent well over 2,000 hours growing my personal brand and helping my clients do the same! Inside this book are proven strategies that will give you the knowledge to kick-start your social media marketing, taking your business and brand to the next level.

When you purchased this book, something GREAT happened. You have helped prevent blindness in 100 children by providing them with a rich source of vitamin A. Not only have you stopped children from becoming visually challenged, but you've also increased their ability to fight infection which will improve their chance of survival from a serious illness.

All of this (and more) has been made possible through my

lifetime partnership with the Global Giving Initiative. B1G1: Business for Good.

I believe that every business has the power to change lives by giving back through its everyday business activities. Doing this together with you is a simple but powerful example of putting this belief into action.

So again thank you; not just for your purchase of the book, but for also making a huge difference in a child's life.

Together, we've made a huge impact.

Adam Houlahan

CHAPTER 1

All the 'whys'

WHY I WROTE THIS BOOK—WHERE IT ALL BEGAN

Back in 2011, I was sitting at my desk looking at market research on the challenges retail businesses were facing and mulling over why most reports showed low sales growth and intense competition—and what the drivers of these issues were. Once I digested this depressing scenario, it was time to look into some of the success stories of the retail industry, and why they were bucking the trend and thriving in a market sector that was generally considered to be experiencing tough trading conditions.

There were numerous reasons that were unique to each company and industry I studied, and one common recurring trend. They all were using Social Media marketing exceptionally well. So it became apparent this Social Media phenomenon needed some further research.

In 2011, I did not have a Facebook account, had never seen a Twitter profile, Pinterest had only just emerged in beta testing and Instagram founders Kevin Systrom and Mike Krieger were toying with their new platform.

To date, more than 4,000 hours of my time have been spent researching Social Media–the more you study it, the more complex it becomes. More than 400 sites exist currently. Which ones are suited to business applications? Which ones will not exist in years to come?

If you have not seen *The Conversation Prism*, it is an infographic that organises Social Media platforms in an effective way–it groups them by how social networks are used by the business world and by the people who are influenced by Social Media to spend their hard earned income. This is a great little tool you should look at regularly. You can get more information at **www.conversationprism.com**. It is always very interesting reading and has evolved over the years with the changing trends.

What became very clear during this research phase was there is no shortage of Social Media outlets. There are dozens of marketing strategies and new trends to use Social Media in the latest sure fire ways almost every month. Facebook dominated the focus of almost every company.

What I could not find was an effective, long-term way to build your own communities of engaged followers who were interested in your brand and happy to be brand advocates and returning customers. So the journey began to find out what were the most effective platforms to use, how to reach out to the right people and, most importantly, how to do this in a time frame that did not take up too much time and distract you from your core business responsibilities.

Roll forward to today, early 2014: I have now built this model to over 200,000 targeted followers across multiple networks. It's easy to follow and takes less than one hour per day. My LinkedIn profile is in the top 1% globally (rated by LinkedIn). LinkedIn uses my profile in its own marketing campaigns as an example of how to structure a great profile.

Google ranks my Google Plus profile in the top 50 profiles in Australia, and I have a Pinterest following currently in excess of 75,000 people (growing by thousands of people every month). I have received numerous offers to purchase my profile, the most recent for in excess of USD $10,000.

The next test was to see if this model could be replicated by other businesses. Which has now been implemented and tested across multiple industries in Australia, the United States and the Middle East.

WHY YOU NEED A SOCIAL MEDIA PRESENCE

The global business world has experienced more upheaval in the last five years than almost any other time in history—but not through recession or government ineptitude. A little phenomenon called the Internet has revolutionised how we buy products, get jobs, research purchases, book holidays and much, much more. It has enabled what were once small or local industries and operators to reach out to the world. No longer do businesses define their competition by geographical boundaries or by a level playing field in which all players are bound by the same rules.

How are these nimble companies achieving their reach to the global community? Social Media, of course, is their weapon of choice. Just think of how much our lives have changed in this short period of time.

Not long ago if you wanted to book a flight, you would call an airline or a travel agent and hope you were getting a good deal or access to all of the available options. Today, almost all flights are booked online through the airlines websites or services such as webjet.com or many other similar websites.

How many of us still use phone books to find a local business? Well, almost all of us, instead of receiving two giant books each year, we use online phone directories.

One of the greatest franchise success stories of the early 21st century was to own a video store. How many stores do you believe will exist by 2020? It is simpler to order a movie online these days without leaving your couch.

We have become conditioned to searching, interacting, researching and purchasing online. Is it any wonder that the smartest businesses and industries are spending huge portions of their marketing budgets online?

One question I get asked almost more than any other by business owners is 'What is the ROI (return on investment) on having a Social Media presence?' My answer is always, 'You get to stay in business.'

Take a look at the top 10 companies in your market sector. How many of them are *not* using Social Media? With the rapid pace at which this online world is growing, how many businesses do you believe will be able to compete and thrive in five years time if they are not using Social Media?

How many of us have purchased something online in the last 12 months from seeing some kind of online advertising or offer?

WHY BUILDING A STRONG FOLLOWER BASE IS ESSENTIAL

THE RETURN ON INVESTMENT

There are plenty of marketing agencies who will tell you they can build you an effective Social Media marketing campaign even if you have no real follower base, and the good ones can. I am certainly not suggesting you should not use these methods. By all means, if you can afford it, you should use them. But what if there was a way you could build over time a really highly targeted audience who knows who you are, trusts in what you say and sell and who will happily spread your message far and wide on a regular basis?

Of course, this is what this book is about. But why is it important? The PPC (pay per click) type of marketing does work. It is just a numbers game—get your message in front of as many people as you can and hope they are interested in what you have to offer, hope they are in the market for what you are selling at that point in time and hope they trust enough in you to purchase from you having had no prior experience with you as a business. It does generate sales, but here is a great example of why business owners ask what the ROI is: it is a simple formula that compares the acquisition cost of a new customer from a sales campaign with the revenue generated. It is possible to spend more on marketing your offer than the campaign generates in profits after expenses.

However, if I have my own data base of highly engaged and trusting followers, at zero cost, I can promote my offer to them and through them to a global audience of potential customers. My ROI is infinitely higher than if I had to pay for a PPC campaign.

CREDIBILITY

Almost all good websites you see today have links to their Social Media profiles. If we are interested in a product a company has to offer, quite often we will click on their profiles and take a look at their Facebook page or LinkedIn or Google Plus profiles. When we find good content and an engaged audience that are liking posts, commenting or retweeting, etc., almost always our perception of the business is heightened.

This is an often misunderstood value of having a good Social Media presence. When we enter a retail store in a shopping centre, our perception of it as a business is based on a number of factors. Is the store clean and organised? Are the sales people friendly and professional? Does the store smell appealing? Do we like the background music that is playing? All these factors come into play before we even look at the products on sale, and often our purchasing decision is made or broken at this point.

When we find a store that does all of these things well and has products we want to buy at reasonable prices, we are likely to spend our money with them over a competitor in the same niche in the same shopping centre. Of course, if they are a really good business, they will get our contact details and email or text or via other means communicate great offers, entice us to join a VIP program or use any of the many marketing tools to keep us as a long-term customer. They will direct us to join them on Facebook, Google Plus, Instagram, or whatever platforms they use.

If we find the content appealing and we enjoyed our experience at the store, it is almost certain we will follow one or more of their online profiles. In a nutshell, they have built their credibility with us to a level where we are highly likely to keep buying from them over and over. Now that we are following them online, they have the ability to keep in contact with us in a subtle way by offering content that we find interesting, even if we just casually glance at it occasionally, which keeps them at top-of-mind every time we are in the market for their products.

Consider another example of a good store that gives us a similar experience upon entering the store, even to the point where we make a purchase, and they even get our email address and occasionally send us newsletters or special offers. But they don't have a good Social Media presence–they don't get us engaged online and we are not seeing great content from them even subtly. How easy is it to forget about this business even if we had a good buying experience? Think back at how many times you have had a great buying experience but have never gone back to that store because you simply forgot about them.

So, how do we build this credibility in the online world? We don't have the ability to present a nice shop front, and there is absolutely no way to connect with our customer through aromas. (The best stores in every shopping centre use this to great effect; the next time you enter a shopping centre, be conscious of the aromas you experience when you walk into different stores and how they affect your perception of them). We have no friendly salesperson to greet the customer each time. It is very easy to find many websites selling similar products or even exactly the same products. So what is it that makes us keep returning to one website over possibly dozens of others selling the same products?

It is the credibility they have built with us, the trust we have in them. And how did they build that trust and credibility? Through Social Media profiles! In the same way we judge a store in a shopping centre, we will form an opinion of a website by how engaged we become with it. How often have you found a product on a website you are interested in and then clicked on their Social Media links to see what they are doing in this space?

You find two sites selling similar products. One has Social Media profiles attached, but when you go to them, there is no engaging content or very few people interacting with posts or–even worse–no content posted for a week or two. The other site has thousands of followers, up-to-date content, and people engaging with the content. Which one are you likely to buy from?

Social Media builds credibility in the physical world and the online world; it is often the single motivating decision that entices your customers to buy from you or from someone else. It is often the difference between whether a customer remains a customer or moves onto a more social-savvy business, simply because they are receiving constant contact subtly from that company's Social Media presence.

INDEPENDENT ENDORSEMENT

How often has your purchasing decision been influenced by a friend or colleague? In years gone by, the only way we were influenced by these trusted people was through a conversation. They may have been wearing something we liked, and we asked where they purchased it. At this point, they can influence us in a positive or negative way. They might give us a glowing endorsement of the purchasing experience, or the opposite.

Today, this is still an important way purchases are influenced; however, now we can also be influenced by seeing content our friends share on Social Media, and we also tend to have much larger networks of people we interact with online than in the physical world. Whilst these people may not be close friends or colleagues, we still become exposed to everything they do online.

The ability to have thousands of people as your brand advocates and become exposed to tens of thousands or hundreds of thousands of potential customers or clients can only be done through Social Media. PPC campaigns or purchasing mailing lists or any of the plethora of other marketing mediums, even online marketing mediums, cannot give you this independent endorsement. It is simply the most powerful opportunity to engage new customers or clients over all other marketing options.

Companies with big marketing budgets use celebrities to endorse their products because they know we are more inclined to trust a successful sporting identity or movie star. You, too, can leverage the power of well known people to your advantage and all in just one hour per day!

WHY ONE HOUR PER DAY

We seem to always be able to find an hour a day if it is for something important enough to us, like going to the gym. If your gym instructor told you he or she could help you lost 10 kilograms in 12 weeks, but you will need to spend three hours every day exercising, he would not have many clients. Just like weight loss programs, building your online presence takes consistent action. There is no value in cramming all of your gym training into five hours one day and then doing nothing until next week. This program is the same—you need to do it every week day.

I have a very hectic work schedule Monday to Friday. I also enjoy going to the gym six days per week and, in my spare time, I have to find time to write books and training courses. On top of all this, my wife has her own small business that keeps her out of the house three nights of every week.

Being time disciplined just has to be a part of my life at all times. My day generally looks like this: Wake at 4 am and write from 4.30 to 5.30 am; gym from 5.45 to 6.45 am; in the office from 8 am to

5 pm. After some family time, I will write for another hour, do my Social Media work for an hour and then read for an hour before bed.

It is very easy to get distracted by our busy lives and decide to give something a miss. I find by having a strong routine, I get everything I want to do done, and my ability to focus very heavily on a task is limited to around one hour. So, it became very important to me to develop this program in a way that would be effective but also limited to one hour per day.

You will also find it has a slow start but gathers momentum. Eventually, you will be gaining more than a thousand new followers across your networks every week. And the more proficient you become at the program, the less time it will take.

Start by deciding when each day suits your schedule best and block that hour out in your calendar every week day for the next six months.

CHAPTER 2

The seven mistakes you must avoid

Let's face it we all make mistakes, especially in business. I have always found there are two great ways to learn anything. The first is by making mistakes ourselves, assessing them, overcoming the set back and getting on with it. The second is by taking the time to learn from the mistakes of others who are good enough to sincerely share them with us.

When I was 23 years old I decided to start my first business, I set about doing some research (a much harder task in 1987 before I even knew how to use a computer). Of course, I told my family and friends what I was planning. Some were supportive and some were not. Everyone was full of advice: some practical, some helpful, and some I could have done without. It is probably still one of the most exciting times of my life I can recall–that planning stage before you actually get into a business–and then reality hits you in the face like a baseball bat.

I still remember the best advice I was ever given during that research phase of my soon-to-be new business, and I still practice it today. At that time, I worked for a holiday resort in Queensland, Australia, taking guests waterskiing, horseback riding, sailing, etc. This particular day I was playing golf with a group of our guests, one of whom was a 60-plus year old self-made millionaire I had known for a couple of years from repeat visits to the resort. I was telling him this was likely the last time we would be playing golf together as I planned to soon leave this amazing job to start out in my first business.

I knew he had owned many businesses, so I asked him for some good advice from his experiences over the years. He gave me this one simple gem.

Go to some cities other than where your business will operate and speak to some people with the same business as you. Tell them you are just starting out and that you would like just one piece of advice: 'What was the biggest mistake you ever made in your business and how did you overcome it?'

I am glad to say I took his advice, and the problems I easily avoided most likely made the difference between me going broke within 12 months and the business thriving as it did.

So, I will admit here and now that I have made every one of the following mistakes in the past.

FACEBOOK IS NOT THE MOST IMPORTANT PART OF YOUR SOCIAL MEDIA STRATEGY

Are you serious? A Social Media book without Facebook?

Yes that is correct. You are not going to find a chapter in this book about Facebook. I have nothing against Mr. Zuckerburg or what is still the number one Social Media platform in the world. I have a great personal profile with thousands of friends and followers, and I use it every day for keeping up with friends and wasting away a little of each day over lunch or after dinner.

I do not spend much time on it building networks of targeted people or interacting with followers for business purposes. You can certainly find plenty of people who are skilled in using it for marketing campaigns or books to teach you how to do that yourself.

Should you have a page for your business? Yes you should, for now most people looking at your Social Media profile will still gravitate towards your page to see what you are about. This book is about building a highly targeted business asset that improves your ability to get your message out to tens of thousands of people at a very low cost. I honestly believe there are just better platforms to do that. I also intensely dislike some features of Facebook that are designed to generate revenue.

One example is the fact that no matter how many people may be following your page, a very low percentage of them will actually get to see your message each time you post information. Unless you meet certain criteria they set or pay to 'boost' your message each time you post. If you pay to boost your message, you can choose to boost it to as many people as you are willing to pay to have potentially see your message.

Of course, the more followers you have, the more you can pay to boost to an even larger audience. You can also use many other features to promote your message or offer—there is no shortage of ways to spend thousands of dollars through Facebook.

If you have the budget for this, by all means use these features. The point is this book is about building 'targeted' followers to utilise for long-term relationship-building at low cost. Facebook just does not rank under these criteria as well as other platforms we will dive into.

This may be a controversial statement, and only time will tell if it becomes a reality. In my opinion, now that Facebook has become a public company and is therefore required to act in the best interest of its stock holders, it will move more and more towards becoming a fully paid service whereby the value you get from your profile will be dictated by how much you are prepared to pay, not by the time and effort you invest into building a high quality following or by sharing great content on a regular basis.

RETURN ON INVESTMENT

We have already lightly touched on ROI; however, it is one of the most common questions asked about Social Media marketing. It is also one of the key points in this book: there is no doubt you can run a marketing campaign that has a negative or very low ROI from a purely numbers point of view.

Ask yourself these three questions:

1. How many of your competitors currently have multiple Social Media profiles?

2. In five years' time, how many of your competitors will be using Social Media to generate significant portions of their revenue?

3. How well do you believe you will be able to compete on the global playing field in five years' time if you do not start investing in your Social Media capabilities now?

From this stand point, it is simply a no-brainer to start building your online presence; however, spending large amounts of your marketing budget until you have built a truly engaged network is not. You may get a good ROI, or you may not. Taking the time at very low cost to start building your network for the future is the best ROI you will ever receive.

USING TRANSACTIONAL MARKETING INSTEAD OF RELATIONSHIP MARKETING

Social Media is all about building trust through relationships, Transactional Marketing certainly has its place, but first you must have the relationships. So how are they different?

Transactional Marketing puts all of the emphasis on getting the sale; it starts with a product your market needs. You have a price enticer, so it may be priced at a discount to get your customers to try it for the first time, or you justify why it's higher than competitors' prices. It is placed in a premium position to catch the eye of your customer. So, on a website, it may be in a banner ad on the home page; in a retail store, it would be near the check out or on the front end of an aisle to gain the most attention. Finally you will have a promotional campaign designed to entice a 'buy now' decision with an enticing call to action.

Your biggest challenge in Transactional Marketing is gaining the attention of the buyer against the constant bombardment they experience. We receive special offers daily, information about the latest and greatest never-seen-before wonder products, never–to-be-repeated prices, and on and on.

Transactional Marketing is a great tool if used in the right environment and at the right time. Social Media can be a great medium to assist with the promotional aspect of these types of campaigns. You either need to spend large amounts of money on campaigns to get your message in front of as many people as possible and hope they are interested in the product at this point in time, or you must have a large network of engaged followers who trust you when you say this is a good product at a good price.

Relationship Marketing, if done right, is one of the most powerful tools in your arsenal. The key is to be giving an exceptional experience to anyone becoming a fan of your business over a long period of time. There is very minimal focus on making a sale or self promotion, and a large focus on solving the problems of your followers with useful *free* information.

Think of it like building a friendship you want to have for years. It is built on trust, respect and mutual value to both parties. You are supplying trusted information that solves your new friends' needs, which they value very highly. In return, your new friends are supplying you with a loyal and independent third party endorsement that shows your business has integrity. They become much more than just potential clients or customers; they become a brand advocate promoting you to all of their family, friends, and connections in the physical and online worlds.

You simply must focus on Relationship Marketing and commit the time and energy required; the reward is the greatest ROI you will ever find. And you get to stay in business!

TAKING A SHORT-TERM APPROACH TO YOUR SOCIAL MEDIA PROGRAM

This is a marathon, not a sprint. The more blogs you subscribe to, the more Social Media newsletters you receive, the more latest fads or 'how I made $30,000 last month from this simple email campaign' type of hype you are going to be exposed to.

That is not to say you should not research new ideas or gain quality information from well respected industry leaders. You should ensure though that you have a long-term strategy in place and that you stick with it over the long term. This is not about extracting the most money out of as many people in as short a time as possible—it is about building trust through relationships.

The strategy that works best for this program is based on Relationship Marketing. If you deviate from a Relationship Marketing program into a Transactional offer too early, you will damage the trust you have been building with your ever-increasing brand ambassadors.

The steps we go through happen in a systemised way to maximise the power of this program. How long this takes is really controlled by you. The more disciplined you are to some daily actions, the quicker the process will be; realistically, this is likely to be a 12-month investment of your time. The rewards if you run the marathon and do not succumb to a sprint are well worth the investment.

POOR BRANDING

Now that you are going to be seen online in many locations, you need to be instantly recognisable. You need to ensure that all of your logos are professional and consistent. When individuals visit your profiles, it is essential they are exposed to the same branding each time. Having a different logo or tag-line on your website to your Social Media profiles sends a confusing message.

Invest some time and money now in getting this right; before you start this journey you must have this in place. If you have a relationship with a graphic designer, talk to them about being clear in the message you want to portray about yourself and your business. It must be consistent across every profile you use, your website and even your email signature. Every time anybody is exposed to you or your business, they must be crystal clear about who you are and what you do.

Your email signature is one of the most underutilised tools to drive people to your many online profiles. Invest in a great-looking HTML signature that links to all of your profiles and your website.

This does not need to be expensive or take a great deal of time to put in place; there are many businesses that specialise in packages for just this purpose. Around $200 should get you a very professional logo, email signature, Twitter background, Google Plus background, and yes, even a Facebook background image. Each needs to be configured to different sizes, so it's best to ensure the company you use are familiar with the sizing requirements for each platform.

Your tag-line needs to be short and clear, and it needs to be on every platform you use.

LAUNCHING YOUR PROFILES TOO EARLY

If you are just starting to use some of these new platforms, don't race out to have links added to your website just yet. A key aspect of your Social Media profiles is credibility; nothing screams lack of credibility more than having nothing on your profiles.

Before you expose them to your existing customers or new people visiting your website, it is best to build them up with some content, future brand ambassadors, comments, etc. first. You should have things looking very professional within 30 days, so keep them off your website until then.

WHAT IS THE MINIMUM TIME FRAME BEFORE WE LAUNCH?

There are not set minimums, but after 30 days you should have at least 50 to 60 posts, tweets, etc. and hundreds of new followers. Personally, I feel 1,000-plus followers says credibility–keep in mind the marathon. Don't rush this small step. Thirty days of consistent content and or 1,000 followers are good bench marks to aim for.

If you have spent months or even years getting to 1,000 followers before, don't worry; we will be getting to the fun part of building that follower base very quickly in the next few chapters

SUCCUMBING TO THE FAKE FOLLOWER TEMPTATION

We have all seen the offers: 'get 5,000 followers for $5' or something similar. It should be obvious that these are fake accounts that will never interact with you or your business. So, if on some level credibility is relative to how many followers you have on your profiles, then why not give it an initial boost with these types of offers?

Almost every business I have worked with has admitted to doing this at some stage early in their online journey. And yes, even I did this early on for my Twitter account. This was before I knew how to build a real follower base. I recall seeing an offer for 10,000 followers within three days. At the time, I had about 2,000 followers, and the temptation to quickly go above 10,000 was too tempting. Of course, within a few days I had almost 13,000 followers; they always deliver a little more than you paid for. At least they understand the value of under promising and over delivering.

My follower-to-follow ratio looked great, but of course my engagement was still what it was with 2,000 followers. I have since removed all of these so-called 'followers' from my account. I now regularly have a clean-up of my account and remove any suspected fake profiles that have followed me. I will show you how to do this in the Twitter chapter.

Real credibility comes from having your followers interacting, commenting, and sharing your content. It is very obvious when you see a Facebook page or Instagram account that has 20,000 or even 100,000 followers but no interaction that these are not real followers.

This program is about building real credibility with real people who love you or your business, are happy to share your great content with their friends and followers, and, importantly, buy what you have to offer. It is better over the long term to have 10,000 real and active people than 50,000 that never have any interaction with you.

At some point, it is highly likely that these people who offer these services will lose interest or get shut down. All of a sudden, you may find all of these fake accounts simply disappear over night from your profile.

Recently, Twitter had a large-scale clean out of inactive accounts. Millions of accounts were shut down and removed from Twitter. Many people found their follower numbers decreased over night by thousands. Personally, I think it was a great move by Twitter, and I hope they do this on a regular basis. Again it is more important to have engaged and active followers than simply numbers of inactive people on your profile.

Real credibility and influence comes from engagement, not from follower counts. Take the time to build your online presence the right way, and you will have a very valuable asset into the future. You will have the best of both worlds: large numbers of followers and real engagement.

CHAPTER 3

Content is king

CONTENT STRATEGY

So what is a content strategy? Ask 10 experts, and expect 11 different answers. Many will argue the difference between content marketing and having a content marketing strategy. Search these terms and then set aside a week to read all the different variations and suggestions.

I am going to attempt to make this very simple.

Your content strategy should be about offering at zero cost useful information that your target market wants to have.

There are just two things you need to focus on: the content must be great, and it must be free. If you can achieve this, you have the winning formula. I have heard many arguments that if you make great information available for free, then nobody will value it; or if I give away my best information for free, then nobody will pay me for my advice.

No matter what industry you operate in, this is almost always incorrect. We live in the age of search engines. It is possible to find the answer to almost any query we have from a simple search. The followers you want to build on your Social Media profiles are looking for a place to get great information about subjects they are interested in.

I have a saying I like to often quote when I am speaking about this topic, and it is 'He who gives away the best information most often wins'. What I mean by this saying is that if you want to build a large following online of targeted brand advocates, give them your best information as regularly as you can. Realistically, this means coming up with one or two gems of advice each week. This is not as easy as it may sound. I suggest starting out with just one article per week and see how it goes. Keep in mind you have to continually create great content. Here are two pieces of advice that will make this a lot easier to achieve.

1. Don't be afraid to offer information to your followers written by other industry experts. If you find a great article written by someone else, share a link to it and tell your tribe why you think this information is useful to them. Offering great information regardless of who created it is a sure fire way to build the trust and respect for yourself or your company.

   If you need validation of this concept, take a look at my Twitter profile. I almost always offer links to information from many sources around the world other than my own. My follower count just grows and grows. I get so many messages from people that I can barely find the time to read them.

2. Be a great recycler. If your information is good and your follower counts are growing, it is likely your new followers have not seen or read articles you wrote months ago. There is nothing wrong with re-sharing your content as long as it is still relevant

today. Mix it up; share some old alongside new. There are no set guidelines, but recycling after six months is a good guide.

START WITH A PLAN

If you start each week trying to decide what you are going to publish and what images you are going to use that week, you are in for a hard road. Always keep in mind this is a marathon not a sprint. If you are going to run a marathon, you don't wake up on a Monday morning and decide this weekend is the time to enter the race. Months of planning, training and preparation will be needed before you will be even capable of running such a distance, let alone be competitive.

Fortunately, we are not attempting to run an actual marathon, but it does pay to be organised well in advance. I would suggest before you even start this journey that you plan a month worth of articles and images. Create a content and posting schedule for your Social Media profiles. It is highly likely you have some work to do getting your branding right before you start; while you are doing this is also the best time to start planning your launch.

There are endless ways to create a posting schedule once you have your content ready. If you are already using Google Plus, one good option is to just create a separate calendar for your content; you can then cut and paste each day's content as required.

A simple excel spreadsheet will also work just fine. Whatever platform you are comfortable with and already using will do. The most important thing is to have a forward plan so you are not scrambling to come up with ideas on the day.

I have tried many versions of how to schedule content; all of them will always save you time in the long run, and it is essential if you want to keep this process to one hour per day. The process I find works best for me is spending 30 minutes of each day researching or creating the content I am going to post. I keep folders for articles or tweets etc. in Google Drive so I can access them anytime from any computer anywhere in the world. I also keep backups in Dropbox just in case anything ever goes wrong with Google Drive. So far, this has never happened. I just like to be well prepared and never want to rely on a piece of computer hardware for storing all of my content.

HOOTSUITE

One of the greatest time savers you can invest in is HootSuite (**www.HootSuite.com**). There is a free version that allows you up to five networks. The pro version is only around $10 per month and allows virtually unlimited networks. It is worth the small monthly fee. There are many other features with the pro version, such as allowing access to team members to assist with uploading content.

You will need to allow some time to initially learn how to effectively use HootSuite. There is a paid service called HootSuite University if you have any difficulties. You will also find plenty of tutorials on YouTube, or you can just search the topic you are struggling with on any search engine. This is well worth the exercise as you will find great tips you never considered possible.

One of the best features you will find is the ability to post to multiple networks in one simple action; for example, you could post the same image to Twitter, LinkedIn, Google Plus and Facebook in one go. You can also forward schedule your posts as far into the future as you like.

There are other platforms similar to HootSuite. I have tried a few but settled on HootSuite as the best value for money and available features. Whatever your preference, forward scheduling is mandatory if you want to have an effective content schedule and not be tied to your computer 24 hours a day, 7 days a week.

If you only have one person taking care of your content scheduling, using HootSuite allows you to plan in advance for holidays. Your content simply continues to roll out uninterrupted all year round.

I strongly suggest you get used to how each platform operates individually and then get used to using a scheduling platform. Some networks have their own scheduling features, which is better than nothing; however, once you get used to a full-featured option like HootSuite, you will save hundreds of hours per year and never miss a day unless you choose to.

At some point you may decide you want to outsource your content scheduling. There are now some very cheap options such as Virtual Assistants or even people on the Fiverr website (**www.fiverr.com**) looking for this type of work and offering very affordable pricing. Of course, if you choose to use these services, do your due diligence on the company or person you are entrusting your businesses reputation to. Regardless of who you have doing your marketing, it is a much safer option to give them access rights through a platform like HootSuite. This way, you never need to give anyone your passwords and live in hope that nothing ever goes wrong. You can have many levels of access; take the time to understand this very important feature before you consider an outsourced option.

We have all heard the saying in any form of marketing that 'Content is King'; it is never more true than in the pursuit of building great online profiles. You can have the best looking website, great branding, and all the Social Media profiles you want; however, if you post images of your dog playing with a stick or, even worse, 'selfies', nobody of any value is going to follow you or interact with your business.

Content refers to two parts of your online posts: the written content and the images that accompany your written words. Every Social Media profile we are going to use relies on images being the core focus of your daily posts.

Even Twitter is rapidly moving from the standard 140 character SMS style tweet to including an image being visible in each tweet. The latest research shows tweets with images are three to four times more likely to be retweeted than tweets with just a link.

It is now imperative that all of your pages on your website include quality images, as well as any blog posts you create. Images improve the readability of your written words and ensure that anybody sharing your content on Social Media is sharing your images by default and improving the reach of your posts. Hopefully you have Social Media share buttons on your web pages and blog posts to make it as easy as possible for people to share your content. These share buttons automatically include your image if you have one somewhere within the article being shared.

There are plenty of free or cheap programs you can get that will assist you in creating great images, infograhics and videos to go with your posts. If you find this part of your marketing challenging, consider using services like Fiverr or Elance to connect with people skilled at this art. You will be surprised how cheaply you can get this work done for you and how fast they work.

Whether you produce your own images or outsource to these services, make including good quality images part of your content strategy as quickly as you can.

Whether you are creating a blog post that you intend to spread via your Social Media profiles or a heading for your Pinterest pins or Google Plus posts, good content is essential. There are two basic 'must haves' that you should follow for great content marketing: the headline and keywords.

HEADLINES

If you can capture attention via your headline and a great image, you will be onto a winning formula. If you need some assistance with how to create great headlines, do a Google search on the term 'Jon Morrow headline hacks'. It is a free download and is 55 pages of pure gold when it comes to creating great headlines.

Generally, these are tips for your blog headlines; however, think a little outside the box on this and use these tips for the short headings on your Social Media posts. Twitter is one of the best platforms for this. You have such a short amount of text to grab attention that your entire tweet is essentially your headline.

I recently saw a tweet that said 'watch this video on why cattle and sheep prefer eating grass' and then a link to a YouTube video. Another one I saw similar to that was 'BREAKING NEWS–Eating grass is awesome'. It does not really matter what the YouTube video was about. Which tweet is more likely to grab your attention?

If you were to additionally promote this video on any of your other Social Media platforms with the option of adding a great image, think of how much more likely someone is to click through to the YouTube video if you had an image of a person with a mouth full of grass than just the standard image from your YouTube video along with the text:

BREAKING NEWS—EATING GRASS IS AWESOME

We only use grass-fed beef in our burgers. Watch this short video to see why grass-fed is better than grain-fed beef.

The key take-away here is to be as creative as possible in your headlines and images. They are a powerful combination that will explode your click-through rates when you put a little effort into them.

HASHTAGS

Hashtags were mostly the domain of Twitter until recently. Now, almost all platforms utilise them. So, what is a hashtag? From a marketing perspective, they are simply a tool to create engagement. Each Social Media platform uses them in its own way. I will give you some basic understanding on each of the platforms we cover in the upcoming chapters. However, some basic fundamentals are a good start. Short is best; keep your tags to fewer than 10 characters wherever possible. Never use spaces, hyphens or special characters like the '$' symbol as these will not work, even if your tag is made up of two words, group the two words as one, such as #SocialMedia. A great place to get some in-depth information about hashtags and what tags are popular on any given day is **www.hashtags.org**.

There are essentially four types of hashtags.

1. *Content hashtags*
   These can be used within the body of your posts and are a great way to improve your Search Engine Optimisation, an example of content hashtags you may use when you post a quote image on Pinterest or Twitter.

If you were to post a quote by Rumi, such as: *You have within you more love than you could ever understand.*

The description of this quote could be: *My favourite #quote by #Rumi*

Content hashtags are supposed to look like a part of the conversation yet link your content to similar posts about the same topics. As is the case with any platform you use, don't over-do hashtags. Three is generally considered a maximum number.

There are many versions of content tags you might use, such as to target a location like #Australia, or even more specific a town or city such as #Sydney. This is a great strategy if you operate from a single location and need to entice people to come to you. A little research into what hashtags your competitors or followers are using is a good way to find the right content tags for your business.

You might use these for a specific event or a particular product. The options are endless; however, keep two concepts in mind:

A) The more generic the hashtag, the wider the audience you will likely reach. Such as #coffee, #car or #quote. If this is your intention, keep them generic; if you need to be more targeted, then drill it down further with an additional tag such as #coffee plus #cappuccino, #car plus #BMW or #quote plus #Rumi. You may need to drill it down even further.

B) The more unique you make a hashtag, the more you will need to promote it to your followers. Unique and generic both have their place, just make sure you use them effectively.

2. *Trending hashtags*

You will find plenty of trending hashtags at **www.hashtags.org**; these are the most popular tags at any given time. They can change by the hour or depending on a particular event or time of the year such as Christmas.

Trends are a great way to get your message in front of a massive audience very quickly. Regardless of how many followers you have, you simply add the trending hashtag to your tweets, posts, etc. Be sure the trend has some relevance to your business before adding trending tags. If there is no relevance to your business, adding the trending tag may be considered spam. Twitter monitors this, and it is technically a breach of their terms and conditions, so you risk having your account suspended.

Twitter makes it very easy to find trending tags; you will see a list of them on your home page on the left side of your profile. Google Plus also has a list that you can easily find in the What's Hot section.

3. *Branding hashtags*

Your brand or business name should have its own unique hashtag that defines who you are. At the start of your Social Media journey, these tags will not have much relevance. However, over time as you become more known, their importance grows. Start using one as soon as you can.

It could be as simple as using your brand name–just add the # at the front and you have your brand hashtag. This is fine if you are the first to use it or if you have a very unique business name. But what if your preferred tag is already in use by another company? If this is the case, come up with another one. Brand tags are required to be very unique, so make sure you do your research before you settle on yours. The simplest way to research whether a hashtag is already getting a lot of use is to just do a search for it on Twitter, Instagram, Google Plus, Pinterest, etc. If your search reveals little or no use of the hashtag, then you are onto a winner. Of course, if you find it well in use, then it is time to get creative and come up with another option.

The same is true with all hashtags: shorter is better where possible, you cannot use spaces and keep in mind the symbols etc that are not supported–do not use these.

4. Campaign hashtags

Campaign hashtags, as the name implies, might be used for a specific event or marketing campaign only. They can be a great way to track results for a specific promotion; however, they can also create some confusion within your brand. There are many marketing people with very different views on the best ways to us these. Personally, I think at this stage of your journey, the focus is on building your follower base, and I would not get too caught up in the use of these tags just yet.

Stick with a brand tag and start experimenting with some content tags for now; there will be a right time and place later for getting more creative.

CHAPTER 4

LinkedIn and the secret sauce

WHY LINKEDIN?

LinkedIn is more about you rather than your business. People like to connect with people as much as with a business or brand. It is simply the best platform to tell your story. Like any other online presence, if you are going to be visible, make sure you present yourself and your business in the best possible way. It is also a very powerful way to promote your business if you use it the right way.

I am going to share with you some great enhancements that are generally not obvious when you first start setting up your profile, some great tips to grow your network beyond people you personally know and associate with **fast**, and how to subtly promote your business to thousands of new connections in just minutes each day.

LinkedIn, whilst it predominantly exists for professionals to connect and network for job opportunities, can be a great way to grow your Social Media presence. However, to do either you need to ensure your profile is maximised to attract the maximum attention from the LinkedIn search engines, which will expose you to the 270 million users currently on LinkedIn. So, whether you are looking to just grow your LinkedIn network or wish to use LinkedIn to grow your other Social Media profiles, follow these simple steps to success.

HASHTAGS

Hashtags are no longer supported by LinkedIn, so don't bother with them in your profile. Whilst it does not seem a sensible move by LinkedIn, hashtags are no different to any other text. You may still see them in use in your news feed as it is likely many people are still not aware of this change.

When I first joined LinkedIn, I knew zero of its potential, and for the first few months would have my profile viewed once or twice a month and would show up in searches two or three times. Since then, I have read literally at least a dozen books or papers on LinkedIn and spent more than 100 hours researching the advice given. As always, some of it was good, some great and some just plain garbage.

Today my profile is viewed hundreds of times every week, it shows up in even more searches and I receive more than 200 connection requests every week. These simple step-by-step guides will fast-track you to bucket loads of views and search results every month and constant growth in your contacts. There are dozens of good strategies utilising LinkedIn to find new customers or clients. If you intend to use it for any of these purposes, you want to ensure your presence is as professional as possible.

YOUR PROFILE

You **must** have a complete profile. The internal search engines within LinkedIn will rank you very low if your profile is not showing as complete. On your profile page on the right-hand side is a profile strength indicator, you want this to be showing as 'All-Star'. This indicates that you have all of the required sections of your profile completed to the required standard. To obtain All-Star status, follow these steps:

A) Upload an image of yourself. _Tip:_ Do not use anything but a head shot of yourself, LinkedIn's terms and conditions require that you use only an image of yourself; adding avatars, logos, etc. can technically be a breach, and you can have your account suspended. However, having a head shot with some colour behind it to stand out is a great idea.

B) 'Name': This is possibly the most underutilised and high-profile section of your profile. By default, it asks you to add your first and last name in two separate boxes. You can put both your first and last name in the first box and an extended description of 'what you do' in the second box. You can use about 50 characters in total here. Use them wisely! Take a look at my profile to get some ideas: au.linkedin.com/in/adamhoulahan.

C) Add a headline. You only have 120 characters, so use them wisely to describe the benefits you offer, and use as close to 120 as you can. Ticks, stars, dots, etc. between topics will make your headline stand out from the crowd. Use these in your headline. A great SEO technique is to add your name again in the headline section.

D) List your current position and at least two others. If you do not have a current or two previous positions, put something 'truthful' in these areas anyway. Leaving these sections blank will ensure you do not reach an All-Star rating.

E) Complete the summary section. This is your chance to expand on the headline. *Tip:* Make this section as interesting as possible. The vast majority of people on LinkedIn make this section so boring, you will be asleep before you finish reading it. The key is to solve the '**NEED**' of your target connections. It is up to you how personal you make this; however, the golden rule is to keep it **'interesting'** and of value to your potential client or customer. This section is the 'make or break' as to whether or not someone will want to take the time to dive deeper into your profile.

Tip: Do not write in the third person for your summary–treat this as your call to action!

Keep in mind that many people may have exceeded their 3,000 connection request limit, so ensure you have your email address here to make connecting as easy as possible.

F) In the 'Skills & Endorsements' section, make sure you have at least 10 skills. Check out other people's profiles that show 500+ connections and make a list of skills to use that are relevant to your profession.

G) Complete the 'Groups' section. All of these terms will hyperlink you to other users with similar interests to you.

They are also search engine rocket fuel. Pick at least five groups of interest to you, and be active in a couple of them. Groups are LinkedIn's best way of interacting with your connections. Unlike Facebook, Google Plus, Instagram, etc, your connections on LinkedIn will rarely respond to posts you make on the home page, which are called updates. _Tip:_ Do not over-do updates; I rarely post more than two or three per day. Do your networking within groups.

So these are the getting-started basics. Check out a few profiles of people with interests similar to yours to ensure you write some compelling but truthful information about yourself; but most importantly, write about the problem you 'solve'. If copywriting is not your strong point, consider using fiverr.com to find someone to help you with this. It will be $5 well spent.

GETTING FOUND

Here are some tips that will improve your profile and search results to look like the LinkedIn pros. If your profile is correctly optimised, it should rank number 1 in searches on Google, Yahoo, etc. like mine.

Depending on what other Social Media platforms, websites, etc you use, the order of these will constantly change in a Google search. Your LinkedIn profile will generally rank in first position (unless you share the name of a famous person like Nelson Mandela). Either way, as far as you are concerned, your LinkedIn profile is likely to rank above everything else. So it makes sense to ensure this is the best representation of **YOU** possible.

A) LinkedIn by default will give you an obscure URL. It is imperative that you update this if possible to your name or how you want to be found by search engines. *Tip:* Try to keep this the same across all of your online profiles; it will ensure all of your online profiles group together in searches. As an example, do a Google search now on Adam Houlahan–you will see my LinkedIn profile usually ranks number 1. This is due to the high volume of searches that happen every week on my profile and it being very search engine optimised. My Twitter, Blog, Pinterest, Facebook, Google Plus, etc. all come up together as well and have thousands of interactions, yet LinkedIn usually rates number 1.

I changed my URL to **http://au.linkedin.com/in/ adamhoulahan**. You should try to change the last section to your name. If this is not available, make it your name plus the number 1 or 2, etc. *Tip:* Try to pick something that you can use across all of your online profiles such as Facebook, Twitter, etc. To do this, go to **Profile** then **Edit Profile.** Click on the **Customise your public profile URL** tab and make the changes.

B) While you are in this section, 'brand' your websites by choosing the 'other' option and using a compelling name for your blog or website. Use anything other than 'My website'. You can list up to three sites here, and I strongly urge you to use a XeeMe profile as number 1. If you do not have a XeeMe profile already, use the below link to set one up now. It is free and allows you to list ALL of your online sites in one easy link. There will be more about XeeMe later. (http://xeeme.com)

1. Add your Twitter handles if you have them. You are allowed more than one, so add any you have. *Tip:* When you look

at other profiles, you will see the Twitter logo but not on your own profile. Don't worry–yours looks the same to anyone else looking at your profile as it shows when you look at theirs. It is just that you are viewing yours as an administrator of your account.

2. Make sure you make your profile visible to the public so anyone can see you. To access this, go to Profile, Edit Profile, and Edit and Tick the tabs for public viewing.

C) You can now embed videos, images or documents into your profile. If you have them, use them! To some degree, you can write whatever you like, but a supporting video, PowerPoint or Slideshare presentation or image of an award or degree gives credibility.

D) Complete as many sections as you feel are relevant to you, such as:

- Experience
- Languages
- Publications
- Test scores
- Courses
- Patents
- Certifications
- Volunteering
- Etc., etc.

However, do not add information for the sake of filling these in; just leave them blank if they are not relevant to you.

E) Optimise the position of each section, keeping in mind many potential connections will just skim the top of your profile before deciding whether to read on or connect at all. So clearly the most interesting information needs to be at the top.

Your image and contact information by default will be at the top and cannot be moved; after that everything is optional. I have tried many versions of positioning information, and the current layout has proven the most successful.

To move the position of each section, go to 'Edit Profile'. Hover over a heading, such as 'Experience', left-click your mouse and then drag the entire section up or down to where you want it positioned. Repeat for each section until you are happy with the order. Save, and you are done.

F) One of the most respected and important features of LinkedIn are 'Recommendations'. This is similar to a written reference. They are a third-party verification of your skills or past achievements. Anyone of your connections can give you recommendations, as you can give them the same. The best way to get recommendations is to 'give' them to others. Be truthful and brief when doing this. It is very easy to give one: when on your contacts profile, you will see a section showing any recommendations they have plus an invitation to supply them with your recommendation. Simply click on this link and follow the step-by-step process.

G) Endorsements, whether you love them or hate them, are now a vital part of LinkedIn for lifting you up the ranks in the advanced search features of LinkedIn. There are many experts with an opinion about the value of endorsements. Personally, my opinion is their greatest value is in their ability to improve your search ranking. Make sure the top 10 are really relevant to your skill set, then get as many as possible for those 10. Only the first 100 will show on your profile for each category, but the more you have, the higher you rank.

As always, the best way to receive is to give–the more you endorse your contacts, the more they will likely endorse you.

BUILDING YOUR NETWORK

At this point, you need to have a clear idea as to how you intend to use LinkedIn–there is no right or wrong. Many people I know like to keep their contacts limited to people they know and interact with on a regular basis. If this is your intention, then be very selective in who you send connections requests to. This next section is how I use my profile and how you should use yours if you wish to massively increase your connections as quickly as possible.

So now that you have your profile set out like a pro, it is time to start building those contacts. I recommend three strategies to do this.

A) **Your own personal contacts**: You may be surprised by how many people you already know are on LinkedIn. The easiest way to find out and make contact is to just import your email list. LinkedIn supports a number of email providers such as Outlook, AOL, Yahoo, Gmail, Hotmail, etc. To do this, go to the **Add Connections** tab inside Contacts and then log into your email and follow the prompts.

There is a high probability that these people who already have some connection with you will be very likely to accept your connection request. Depending on how many contacts you have, I would suggest sending connection requests in batches of no more than 100 at a time. Since you already know these people, you will want to respond to each one who accepts your request with a short note thanking them for accepting your request. Have a short reply already drafted that you can copy and paste each time and just insert the first name of the respondent each time. Make sure you also do them a little favour and endorse their skills—it will only take you a minute, and most people reciprocate the favour, which drives activity on your account every day.

LinkedIn will only show a progressive count of the first 500 connections you have. Once you reach 501 regardless of how many more connections you have it will show the number as 500+; however, you can have up to 30,000. LinkedIn does this to stop the competitive nature of having more contacts than anyone else. Many people get around this limit by displaying the number of contacts they have in their headline. The headline is very valuable real estate for searches; don't waste this space displaying how many connections you have—nobody really cares!

B) **XeeMe:** You should have a XeeMe account. If not, go to XeeMe.com and set one up now.

XeeMe is changing its branding and will likely eventually just be known as Society 3. You will see both names when you navigate to their site. Whilst XeeMe is attempting to be a Social Media platform in its own right, its greatest value has always been the ability to showcase all of your Social Media profiles in one easy to share location. You can share one link to your XeeMe profile instead of individual links for each and every profile you use.

You will find that literally thousands of people on XeeMe have a LinkedIn account. Anyone on XeeMe is open to accepting your connection request on not only LinkedIn but almost any site you use. If you use Facebook, there is a great group called XeeMe Power Networker Group. It is an invitation-only group of very active networkers. Once you set up your XeeMe account, request an invitation to this group.

Tip: LinkedIn allows you to send only 3,000 connection requests. Once you exceed this number, it is still possible to send more, but it's much harder. It does not matter whether people accept your connection request, the 3,000 limit still applies. Once you have exceeded 3,000, you will need the email address of the person you are attempting to send a connection request to. You want to make sure a high number of your connection requests are going to be accepted. This was the biggest mistake I made in the early days on my account as I exceeded this number and only averaged a 30% acceptance rate when I was sending invites. Using your own contact list and XeeMe will increase your acceptance rate to above 70%. If I knew this when I started, I could have averaged around 90% acceptance rate!

THE SECRET SAUCE

This is the 'golden goose' for growing your network on LinkedIn, and the best part is all you will have to do each day is log into your account and accept as many connection requests as you like. I receive between 150 and 200 per week.

This will cost you a one-time fee of around $50 for the year, but it is the best $50 you will ever spend. From the day you join, you will receive a constant flow of connection requests from all over the world. The best part is none of these counts toward the 3,000 limit as they are contacting you, not you contacting them. This is a site called Top Linked; to access it just type this link into your browser.

http://www.TopLinked.com.

Top Linked also has a free service you can use; however, the free service requires you to send connection requests–you cannot receive requests. You may want to try this out before paying your annual fee. You will receive acceptances, and it is very easy to upload a CSV file to LinkedIn and send these requests in bulk. I found I received about one in three acceptances; in other words, if you send 300 requests, you will receive around 100 acceptances. This sounds great, but you will quickly use up your 3,000 limit for around 1,000 acceptances. I suggest sending around 1,000 requests in groups of 100 and then utilising the rest of your limit through XeeMe.

There is no obligation to accept any connection requests you receive via Top Linked or any other request. You can pick as many as you choose, and you can be very strategic as to which industries you want to accept requests from. I accept requests from many different industries and have made amazing connections to people that have been able to assist me in many different endeavours. Again, there is no right or wrong; it is up to you how you build your network.

So there you have the simple steps to LinkedIn success. Follow them and you will have a massive network–or a very targeted one–before you know it, search engines hitting your name literally thousands of times forever more and massive growth potential for any other profiles you maintain.

GROWING ALL OF YOUR NETWORKS WITH LINKEDIN

So now you have literally hundreds of new connections coming to you every week via LinkedIn! It makes sense to leverage your new network to join you on Twitter, Facebook, Pinterest, Google Plus or any platform you use. It is always good practice to acknowledge someone who has taken the time to request a connection with you. If you are going to make contact with them, why not offer the opportunity to join you on other networks and give some great free advice at the same time.

For every connection request received, send them back a short reply along the lines of:

Hello 'first name',

Thank you for the invitation to connect with you. I am pleased to accept and honoured to have you as part of my LinkedIn network.

I hope you won't hesitate to contact me if there is anything I can assist you with in the world of Social Media. If you don't already have a copy and would like me to send you my LinkedIn Optimisation Tutorial absolutely FREE, just ask and it is yours. This is the process I used to get my profile to the top 1% of all 250 million profiles currently registered.

I have met many wonderful people by open networking here on

LinkedIn. Please also feel free to connect on any of these sites if you use them—I would be equally honoured to accept such a connection.

http://xeeme.com/AdamHoulahan

By the way, if you use any other sites apart from LinkedIn and you have not seen XeeMe before, take a look at this great free tool. I have found it invaluable for offering to connect on all of my sites from one easy location. Click on this link to set up your own free account, and please do not hesitate to contact me if you need any help with it.

http://xeeme.com

Sincerely,

Adam.

Once you have written your own version of this response you can simply copy and paste it to every connection request you send (just personalise each person's name each time). It will only take you a few minutes each day, and you will grow all of your networks from this one simple greeting.

Don't forget to go to their profile and give them some endorsements while you are there. When you accept a request, a link will appear allowing you to send that person a message.

Tip: If you can offer a free download one relative to your industry, you will become a valued connection on LinkedIn. Take the time to write something you are happy to give away **FREE.** This is your opportunity to position yourself as an expert in your field, and the offer of a free white paper, e-book or whatever works for your industry opens up your ability to create engagement and again get a valued marketing message shared. Always ensure you include a reference to your website and a compelling reason why someone should click a link to your site and interact further. This could be where they get an extended version of your free information, or possibly another free offer. The key is to drive people to your site at all times.

So that is it, if you want to optimise your LinkedIn profile and other networks, gain new connections on your other Social Media profiles and drive traffic to your website, just follow these steps one after the other. If you prefer to keep your LinkedIn profile small and manageable, that is okay, too. Just use steps 1 and 2 to ensure you have a professional profile that stands out from the crowd.

CHAPTER 5

Pinterest and the secret sauce

Have you joined the Pinterest phenomenon yet? Here are compelling reasons why you should!

1. There are now more than 70 million Pinterest users. Considering the site was launched in March 2010, this is incredible growth.

2. People making purchases via Pinterest outrank all of the top five Social Media sites, with four times more revenue per click than Twitter and 27% more than Facebook.

3. Monthly page views now top 2.5 billion, so is it any wonder the conversion rates from Pinterest traffic is a staggering 50% higher than all other traffic?

4. 80% of all pins on Pinterest are repins, so the likelihood of getting your content shared is huge.

The facts are you simply cannot ignore Pinterest any longer as an integral part of your Social Media program. Of course, knowing the facts and knowing how to use Pinterest are two vastly different things. Start by being clear on what your intentions are for logging in every day. If you are using Pinterest for your brand or business, then it is as simple as using it to drive traffic to your website. This is the essence of how Pinterest is used for business: the ability to embed a URL into every post and direct the person viewing your pin to any website you choose. Having a clear strategy will set you on the path to Pinterest success.

SETTING UP A PINTEREST ACCOUNT

Getting started on Pinterest is a very simple process. First, you need to decide if you are going to set up a personal account or a business account. In most cases, you should have a business account. If you're an established brand, small business, non-profit organisation, blogger or publication, you can join Pinterest as a business. If you already have a personal account, you can convert it to a business account anytime. Just follow these steps

To sign up as a business, go to the help centre on Pinterest and to the page Business Accounts. Here is what you will find:

1. If you have a personal account, log out of it.

2. Go to Pinterest for Business.

3. Click **Join as a Business.**

4. Select the type of account, the name and email of the person managing the account and choose a password.

PINTEREST AND THE SECRET SAUCE

5. Enter in your business name, the username that will determine your Pinterest URL, your logo, a description and your website.

6. Read and accept the Business Terms of Service and click **Create Account.**

To convert your existing account:

1. Log in to your account.

2. Go to Pinterest for Business.

3. Click **Join as a Business.**

4. Follow the steps above to set up your account.

5. Click **Convert.**

CHOOSE A BUSINESS ACCOUNT TYPE

Right now, the business type you choose when creating your business account will help us get to know you better. It won't affect the features of your account or your experience on Pinterest. Choose the category that best represents your business. You can always change this option later by going to the Settings page.

YOUR BOARDS

You are allowed as many boards as you like on your profile. For the greatest advantage, make sure your main boards are laser targeted to a specific category within your business and are listed at the top. For example, a wedding planner would have boards specific to wedding cakes, floral decorations, make-up tips, honeymoon destinations, wedding vows, menu ideas, dresses for brides, bridesmaid outfits, gift ideas... the list is endless. The point is to make certain that every board stays focussed on your niche. Keep in mind that the more boards you have, the more time you will need to devote to your profile. The best way to decide what types of boards to set up is simply to search your industry on Pinterest and see what the companies with good follower numbers and repins on their boards are doing.

PIN LIKE A PRO

Here are some golden rules to follow when you upload a pin:

A) Ensure you are pinning the right content to the right board. It is easy when you have multiple boards to get this wrong. If you pin something to the wrong board, you can just hit edit and move it to the correct board. Check all of your pins once you have finished a round of pinning and make sure everything is where it should be.

B) Hashtags work the same as Twitter. Use them. Don't go crazy with them, though, or your pins will look like spam. I find two or three hashtags works best. More than that turns people away. Keep hashtags relevant to your industry and your board. Our wedding planner mentioned above would use the hashtag #wedding on all pins, but #weddingvows exclusively on pins for a board about wedding vows.

C) Try to keep your pin description relevant and short. Pinterest is a visual experience, not the place to outline your life story–that's what your website is for. Craft one or two strong sentences to entice your audience to want to see and read more.

D) Embed your URL in *every* pin! The whole point of Pinterest is to drive traffic to your website. This is a two-step process. First, you must upload your pin. Second, you must edit the pin and add the URL in the 'source' section. Make sure you use the full address

http://www.adamhoulahan.com, not **www.adamhoulahan.com**. If your pin is about a specific section of your website, direct traffic to where you want the person to end up, not to your home page.

E) Everyone hates spammers. You don't want to bombard your followers with constant pins. Anything more than 60-minute intervals is bordering on too much.

CONTENT

In Pinterest terms, content refers mainly to the images you pin, as well as the text. Just like the rest of your Social Media strategy, content is king. Pin garbage and you'll lose your followers.

Pinning is a potential minefield. It's common for pinners to find content in many locations, including Pinterest, Facebook, Google Plus, Flickr, and Pin It with links to their websites. When you pin, be sure to give photo credit where possible to the original owner. Also, use your own images or approved images from your supplier, your website, previous marketing campaigns, etc., wherever possible. Plenty of websites allow you to download royalty-free images.

Great content on the wrong board is a losing long-term strategy. Furthermore, consistently coming up with fresh content is a struggle. A win–win solution is to create one generic board not targeted to your niche and to bury it at the bottom of all of your boards. Now you can regularly pin content to your generic board. This way, if you have a day with no time to pin new content, you can repin gems from your other boards and virtually give them a second life. Avoid repinning to your niche boards to keep them tidy and flowing with new content.

All of your pins should be watermarked with your logo and or website URL–the objective is to get your pins repinned as often as possible. Watermarking ensures your brand is seen as often as possible. Another good option is to include some text overlayed on the Image with your message; just don't go too far and ruin the visual value of your pin.

COMMUNITY BOARDS

One of the best ways to turbo-charge your reach is to get invited to community boards relevant to your niche. Community boards are just like personal boards except that other pinners are allowed to contribute. If you accept an invitation to a community board, that board will appear on your profile.

The power of a community board is that while your personal account may be new and you have zero or few followers, the community board may have thousands of followers. Every time you pin to the community board, you are exposing your content to every follower. Here is one of my best community boards: **http://www.pinterest.com/ adamhoulahan/inspirational-quotes/**.

As you can see, this board has 40,000-plus followers and over 1,300 pinners. Many of the pins get repinned dozens of times as this community is very active. Also, a lot of the pinners are companies that sell or promote products that have nothing to do with quotes. This is the incredible power of community boards, and I strongly suggest you use them as part of your strategy. No matter what industry you are in, it will benefit you to have a quotes board of your own and to request an invite to my board or others like it. Currently, the hottest topics on Pinterest are boards about Do It Yourself projects and quotes, so if your business in anyway promotes DIY projects, then by all means focus on this; if not, quotes are a universally loved niche almost any business or brand can use. A good example is Nike. How many motivational quotes featuring sports people wearing Nike shoes have you seen?

Setting up community boards of your own is the best way to create massive traffic and followers to your profile. You'll want to maintain full control of your niche boards and use only highly targeted pins, so don't make them community boards. For example, our wedding planner profile might have a community board for happy couples to pin wedding photos. All new brides love to show off their wedding photos, and this type of community board gives them the opportunity to do so. Our wedding planner could offer invites to clients, which builds an army of happy pinners pinning free testimonials of the services. For even more exposure, our wedding planner could also open up community boards to non-clients. A word of caution! Doing this might open up the potential for invited pinners to promote a competitor. Our wedding planner, like you, would want to make sure to post specific rules in the board description and enforce them by removing offending pins and any pinners who continually break the rules.

It is easy to spot a community board. Just look for the symbol of three people in the top right corner. You can also search using a term relevant to your niche. Our wedding planner might use 'community board weddings'. In the top left corner of your Pinterest profile is a search bar; just enter your search term and then default the search to boards as opposed to pins or pinners.

GAINING FOLLOWERS

So now you are pinning regularly with great content. You are even getting a few repins and likes on your pins, but very few followers.

Gaining new followers to your profile is as simple as following the people following the boards of other pinners in your niche. Our wedding planner, for instance, would search for quality boards relevant to weddings and follow those boards. If the followers of this board are interested enough to be following this board, they are highly likely to be in your target market. The more global your business, the more beneficial this strategy is. The amount of followers you want to attract and the time you have to devote to growing your Pinterest visibility to your target market is up to you. I suggest you start by following 50 to 100 people per day. You should average about 30 people following you back for every 100 you follow. That means about 10 to 15 minutes of work per day should result in 200 to 300 followers per week. The key is to follow the right people!

To get started, click on the word **followers** on your chosen board and you will see all of the followers of that board. The key to getting a lot of followers is to follow people who are following more people than are following them. When you look at someone's Pinterest profile, in the top left corner you will see two boxes: one is showing their followers, and the other is showing who they follow.

If the profile you are looking at has 1,000 followers but is only following 100 people back, chances are this person won't follow you either. If, however, they have only 280 followers but are following 1,451 themselves, this person is highly likely to follow you as well. It doesn't really matter the number of people the person you choose to follow is following, but generally the less they have following them, the more likely they will be to follow you back.

You have clicked on the word **followers** on your chosen board and are looking at the followers of that board. Now you'll want to scroll down the list and follow these people by clicking the **follow** button under their profile. The more regularly you do this, the quicker your follower numbers will increase–50 to 100 per day is an easy number to achieve.

On many other Social Media Platforms like Twitter or Google Plus you have limits on how many people you can follow at any time. Twitter uses a ratio method; for example, if you have 5,000 people following you, then you can only follow 5,000 plus 10%, so 5,500. Google allows you to follow only 5,000 maximum, regardless of how many people are following you. There are no ratio limits or maximum limits on Pinterest like there are for Twitter and Google Plus. You can follow as many people as you like. Once you are known as a follower of these boards, other people will follow you, too. Return the favour and follow them back. The more you do, the more people will continue to follow you.

Give it a try today and watch your followers multiply.

Another option if you simply want quantity over quality is to use services like Pinwoot (**www.pinwoot.com**). Connecting your account to a service like this will guarantee an increase in followers. However, it is much harder to gain followers who are totally aligned with your niche. Pinwoot uses a currency known as 'seeds', and you earn seeds by following other people's profiles. You can then offer your seeds to other people to follow you. If you do not want to spend a great deal of time following people's Pinterest accounts to earn seeds, you can also purchase seeds and you will get daily followers without doing the work of following people yourself. It depends on what is most important to you—engaged followers or a certain number of followers. There is no doubt that it never hurts for your profile to have a lot of followers, so you might initially use these services to gain momentum and then switch to attracting only the type of followers you really want.

THE STRATEGY

A great way to track your progress is a free service called Tailwind (**http://analytics.tailwindapp.com**). Tailwind will show you how many new followers you received in the past week and how many pins you personally pinned, how many times pins on your profile were liked by other people and—the most important statistic—how many times your pins were repinned by other people.

Even though there are dozens of strategies promoted for using Pinterest, I suggest you start by assessing your time commitment each day. The more time you invest in Pinterest, the better and quicker your results will be.

DAILY TASKS

1) Create 3 new pins and mix them up between your boards, always making at least one a quote. Be sure to insert your website or company name into the image.

2) Like 20 to 30 posts from your followers or people you are following. To do this, just scroll through your feed—any pins showing here are from the people you follow. Your feed on Pinterest is similar to Facebook: to access it, go to the icon

next to the search bar in the top left-hand corner. Once you click on this, it will give you a menu with many options to search through.

The first option is your feed. This shows everything that the people you are following have pinned recently. All of the other options will show pins by everyone using Pinterest, for example, on the topic of education. These are not from your followers, specifically.

3) Comment on five pins using same process as liking outlined in Daily Tasks #2. Just scroll through your feed and leave a positive comment under any pins you liked.

4) Repin five pins to your non-niche board. A great option is to repin the pins you have commented on in above Daily Task #3. The previous three steps are about being social and supporting your community. If you are seen to be active and repinning, commenting, etc., people are more likely to follow you or follow back.

5) Send out 20 invites to your community board or boards. To do this, click **edit** on your board where you will see the field 'who can pin'. In this field, type a letter of the alphabet, such as 'A'. Every person you are following whose name starts with 'A' will pop up. Just click on their name and an invite will be sent.

This is a proven method tested by more than 100 people. All have had great success in building a Pinterest account and getting massive visits to their websites, blogs, etc.

PINTEREST ETIQUETTE

Follow these basic common courtesies to be a good Pinterest citizen:

Give credit where credit is due. If you use someone else's image, acknowledge them where possible. It is always best to use your own or royalty-free images where ever possible.

Everyone hates spammers, especially on community boards. Don't over-do it. Many community boards will have rules set by the creator as to how many times or what content you can pin to these boards. If they are very good boards, the stricter the creator is likely to enforce their rules.

Your own followers will also be turned off if they are seeing hundreds of pins from you every day in their feed.

Be social, repin, follow back and comment. Unless you have a profile that many people just want to be a part of or are a celebrity of some description, the more social you are, the more likely people are to want to engage with you.

Ensure your links match the pin description. Your followers will hate being misled by the description you apply to a pin if it is not aligned with the image you have pinned or the website it redirects to. As an example, if the description you add below your image is referencing healthy home recipes for a toddler and the website link goes to site selling hair removal products, then clearly people viewing your pin will be unimpressed and unlikely to view any more of your pins.

THE SECRET SAUCE

If you follow the steps above, you will be a master of Pinterest in no time at all. I suggest you start out by following this step-by-step process so that you fully understand how to use Pinterest in a very powerful way. No other network can effectively drive traffic to your website or to links you wish to promote like Pinterest can.

Once you have mastered these daily tasks, you can purchase some very powerful software that can automate everything outlined above. Using this software enables you to have Pinterest on autopilot 24 hours a day 7 days a week. Once per day you can set it to do all of the above tasks for you, and your ability to drive traffic to your chosen destination (your website, Affiliate links, a book you have on Amazon or many other web-based locations) goes into hyper drive. Below is the software I use to get so many repins, likes etc. on my account.

Keep in mind that all software has limitations. you will not be able to be as targeted as the process just outlined for following and liking; however, you will be able to get a much larger coverage over any 24-hour period in the number of people you follow or the number of pins you like and how many pins you can pin in a day.

You can purchase it from **www.ninjapinner.com**.

There are great tutorials provided and software updates with new and improved features are always free. You can also try it out free for a couple of hours. It is currently only available for windows-based computers.

As with all of these programs, I am only focussing on how you grow your follower base. Once you have purchased Ninjapinner and have downloaded it to your computer, this is the daily routine that you should follow:

1. Log into Ninjapinner. On the left side of the screen are the menu tabs; open the tab 'Gather Pin/ username IDs'.

2. You should have a list of accounts that you have found in your niche with good numbers of followers. In the URL bar at the very top of your screen, type in the URL of the account you want to auto-follow everyone following this account. If you were going to follow everyone following me, you would type the URL **http://www.pinterest.com/adamhoulahan**.

3. Click on the followers tab for the account, and the screen should populate with the profiles of all of the people following this account. On the far right of the screen, you should see a rectangular tab that says 'Start gathering IDs'. Click on this tab, and you will see the section below that says 'Gathered' start to fill with all of the account profiles you are going to follow.

4. Once this has finished importing all of the accounts, go to the menu tab above 'Auto-Follow / un-follow'. You will see a box that has the number of accounts you have imported. For example, it may say a number like 4,565. This is how many accounts are ready to be followed. The limit Pinterest allows you to follow per day is believed to be 300. I suggest setting this number to 295 each day. Then just click 'Start Following' and let Ninjapinner do the rest for you.

This should only take you a few minutes each day. Pinterest does not seem at this point to have a maximum number of profiles

PINTEREST AND THE SECRET SAUCE

you are allowed to be following. All Social Media platforms are constantly updating how they operate, so I suggest that once per month you use the 'Unfollow' feature to unfollow any accounts that have not followed you back.

This is quite self explanatory: just click on the same tab 'Auto-Follow / Unfollow' and then instead of 'Follow', click 'Unfollow'. An enlarged screen of options will open up. Click the first option: 'Unfollow' users on your Following Page and then, the third option, 'Only unfollow users who aren't following me back'. You should also click the last option, 'Exclude users followed less than x days ago'. I would set this to five days to allow the most recent people you have followed time to follow you back.

Again, like all of the other programs you are going to use, Ninjapinner has many more features than just following and unfollowing. Take the time to master this software and its many features and Pinterest will become a 'must have' marketing tool you will love.

CHAPTER 6

Twitter and the secret sauce

I must admit I was of two minds on the value of Twitter. It was one of the first platforms I started using, and I often questioned its value. I spent a lot of time trialling different strategies, and of course each needed some months to be able to gauge their effect. At one point, I did lose interest altogether and just automated responses and posts so I did not have to worry about it.

I am a major fan of it now that I have found a strategy that suits me, so stick with it. It does take some time to gain momentum, and it will seem like nobody is listening to you even though your follower base is growing.

The best lesson I learned from losing interest in Twitter and automating everything was in regard to automated responses. There are lots of tools available that allow you to automatically reply to someone that follows you. Some even allow you to rotate a number of responses so that not every single response is the same.

My advice, speaking from this experience, is do **not** use automated responses–nothing screams insincerity more than these. I get between 150 and 200 messages per day on Twitter, and 90% are clearly from automated programming. It becomes very obvious after a while and is a major turn off to people interacting with you. I know this because apart from finding it incredibly annoying myself, I started receiving almost abusive return messages from people I had sent automated responses to.

With that little gem of advice, let me show you how to grow your follower base the right way.

CREATING A TWITTER HANDLE

Your Twitter handle is Twitter's version of a username; it defines who you are or what you do on Twitter. It can be anything you like as long as it is a maximum of 15 characters in length. You cannot use spaces or characters, and it must only be letters and/ or numbers. The only exception is the underscore symbol. It will always be precluded by the '@' symbol. My Twitter handle is my name: @AdamHoulahan. If I wanted to separate my first and last name, this is where the underscore is used instead of a space. So I could have @Adam_Houlahan as long as it is not more that the allowed 15 characters, not including the @ symbol.

You can change your handle at any time, so if you already have one and you are not happy with it, or you change your mind later, just go into your settings and make the change. Keep in mind that if you do change it, you may have to update your business cards, letterheads, HTML signatures, links from your website and possibly other places too. So, think carefully about the effects before changing yours.

Twitter also reserves the right to take back a handle if it infringes on a registered brand name or business name that you do not own, so be careful in how you choose your handle. Of course, it must also be unique and not already registered.

If you are using your own name, like mine, as your handle, it is quite possible that someone else of the same name has already registered it. This will not preclude you from having your name in the profile section. You can have up to 20 characters and spaces in this area. You could also try using the underscore if the other person has not used one.

YOU MUST HAVE A PROFESSIONAL PRESENCE

Just like we went through in the LinkedIn chapter, you must have a complete and professionally presented account to stand out from the crowd. There are four key ways to ensure your account looks like the pros' accounts.

1. *Background images*

   There are three areas where you can add branding on your profile. The central image is often your head shot or business logo. You have only a space of 73×73 pixels, so use it wisely. Ensure if you are using a head shot that it is a clear image without any clutter in the background. If you are using a logo here, it will need to fit into a square very well—you may need to have a graphic designer assist with this. Personally, I feel the next section is the best option for a logo. I would always advise using an image of yourself in this section.

   There is a larger section behind this image that allows you to upload a file no larger than 2MB. You cannot stretch or heighten your image, and it will be justified to the top left-hand corner. You access this section by going to your settings and then 'design'. As you will see, in this section you can play around with background colours, font colours, etc. as well. Choose a theme that suits your business or personal taste. Again, it can be worth the small expense to have some assistance from a graphic designer with an 'eye' for this type of detail. This section will also display all of the information that you add to the profile section found in your settings page. It will be overlayed on the image.

You can also have an additional larger branding opportunity that displays to the left and right of the main body of your profile. This section is difficult to get right as it will view differently on different size computer screens. Unless you are very savvy with layout and the intricacies of this section of Twitter, this area is best done by a professional who has formatted images for this area before.

Hopefully you have your branding imagery already done; if not, make sure you get this done before you commence the secret sauce steps in this chapter. If you want thousands of people to be following and engaged in your content, your profiles need to present a very professional image.

2. *Website*

Ensure you have your website added to your profile; however, you can also add another link as part of your bio. This is a great opportunity to add a link to any other online presence you want to direct people to. In both instances, ensure you use the entire address including the 'http://' before the 'www'. On your profile, these will appear without the 'http://www', adding them though is how you create a link directly to your website, etc.

3. Bio

You have 160 characters to use in your bio. This is your opportunity to be very clear regarding what you are about. If you can add your name or company name into the bio, you get some additional SEO value from the searches that take place on your profile. Use this area to be as 'to the point' as you can, but make it very clear what you do, and of course to add a second link to another online profile apart from your website.

4. Keywords

Try to include a couple of keywords in your bio that are specific to the niche you will be tweeting about. Getting this right is not always easy. Keywords are a good addition, but remaining clear in your description is paramount. Otherwise, you appear to be keyword 'stuffing'. Ask some colleagues or friends if your description seems professional. If you have access to a copywriter or can afford to engage one, do so. You can use the same or similar version across multiple networks, so it is money well spent.

STICK TO YOUR NICHÉ

I find Twitter works best when you remain highly targeted to a niché. My niches are Social Media and quotes. So most of my tweets are about Social Media tips with links to great articles. Once a day, I will post a quote and always an image quote. Twitter is rapidly evolving from its roots of the 140 character SMS-type tweet to displaying images in tweets. All of the latest research points towards higher engagement when you have images in your tweets. This is quite understandable given the significant data that exist for almost all other platforms showing much higher engagement when images are included in posts.

I use Twitter to provide my followers with the best possible content available, no matter who writes it. Of course, if you have plenty of great content on your blog, then by all means tweet links to your blog article. There is no down side to tweeting links to old blog posts you may have as long as they are still relevant today. It is a great way to drive traffic to your site and land it on different sections of your site, which helps your SEO, too. Search engines like to see that visitors to your site are going beyond just your home page, so Twitter is a great way to get that mix of views across all of your pages.

If you have a number of topics you want to build a following in, then you will need to be very specific in your use of hashtags or, better still, have more than one Twitter account. I have tried a number of strategies over the last few years, from tweeting 50 times per day across multiple niches to tweeting jokes and other fun, light-hearted or inspirational posts and everywhere in between as far as number of tweets per day and content type. What works best is to stick to a very narrow niche and only a handful of tweets per day.

Over a long period of time, it gets difficult to create or find really high-quality content to keep sharing with your followers. Of course you can and should keep a spreadsheet with your best tweets as long as they will not quickly become out-dated, and you can re-share this content every couple of months. You will be gaining new followers constantly, so it is highly likely your new followers have not seen some of your older content.

Avoid tweeting just for the purpose of tweeting; your followers will not enjoy being spammed. I found when I was tweeting 30 to 50 times a day; I was losing followers and new followers unfollowed after a short period.

HASHTAGS

Hashtags are a useful part of Twitter, but avoid using too many. Two or three are all you need, and ensure they are very relevant to your topics. As an example, I will almost always use the hashtag #socialmedia–the exception being for the one quote I tweet each day. On this, I use #quoteoftheday. A secondary hashtag I might use if the link is going to a blog post about using video content in your strategy would be #video. One of your goals is to have your links retweeted, so too many hashtags makes your tweet look like spam and is less likely to be retweeted.

Keep in mind you only have 140 characters to use. It is also a good idea to allow for the person who is sharing your tweet to have some characters left to add a small amount of their personal content or their own hashtag. I would suggest keeping your characters from 100 to 110 if possible to allow for your re tweeters to add a little of their own content.

LISTS

The more people you follow, the more difficult it becomes to keep track of the good quality and interesting articles you would like to see. The solution is to set up lists on your profile. Through the use of lists, you can organise the accounts you follow into easy-to-view categories. You can have up to 500 lists and 5,000 accounts per list. I suggest you keep to much smaller numbers of accounts in each list, or it almost defeats the purpose.

You might choose to have a list of your clients to keep up-to-date with what they are doing and saying–or of your competitors for the same reason. You could also have lists to research a topic; for example, you could quickly access good content on marketing on Twitter. There are endless ways to use lists, and it is the most effective way to keep track of accounts you are following.

With this in mind, you might now better understand why you should keep your tweets highly targeted to a specific niche. If your content is great, and your followers want to keep a close eye on what you tweet, they are highly likely to put you into a list of their own. How many lists you are on is a great way to gauge how well your content is being valued by your followers. Currently, I am in over 600 lists, almost all of them on Social Media.

HOW MANY LISTS ARE YOU ON?

You can keep track of how many lists you are on by going to your profile and into the lists section; then, click on 'member of', and every list you are on will be displayed.

When you start getting onto hundreds or thousands of lists, it can be a very slow process to see all of the lists you are on. A great free service you can use to quickly see how many lists you are on is called Tweetdeck, Just go to **www.tweetdeck.com** and attach your account. Tweetdeck does many more functions than just show you how many lists you are on. Personally, I don't use these features; I use HootSuite. To see how many lists you are on or anybody else you are following, just click on your name, and a pop up screen will appear showing how many followers you have, how many people you are following and how many lists you are on.

SETTING UP A LIST

Setting up your lists is very easy, go to 'lists' on your profile. To the far right, you will see the tab 'create list'; click on this, and a pop up screen will appear. Here you add the name of your list. This will be visible on your profile if you choose to make it a public list; if you intend to make it public, ensure it is appropriately named. You can use up to 25 characters on the name. If you choose to, you can also describe what the list is about in fewer than 100 characters.

Repeat this process for all of the lists you choose to create; or, if you decide to create a new one at a later time, just come back to this section and repeat this process anytime.

Adding accounts to your lists is just as easy.

Go to the profile of any account you want to add to a list by clicking on the account name. Click on the icon to the left of the 'Follow' button in the right corner. A pop up screen will appear; click on add or remove from lists, your lists will appear and click the list you want to add them to or remove them from.

Once you start using lists, you will find them to be the most efficient way to organise the accounts you follow.

THE SECRET SAUCE

The same as with every other platform, the secret to getting thousands of followers is to simply follow thousands of other people that you want to have follow you. The easiest way to find the right type of followers is to just make a list of Twitter accounts that have huge follower numbers in the same niche as you. As an example, if you wanted to build a follower base interested in tips on Social Media, you could just go to my profile and start following the people following me. You would have a data base of 50,000-plus people who are highly likely to be interested in this niche.

Keeping in mind your content is the key. The people following me will be used to receiving good quality information about Social Media. Unless you will also be tweeting about Social Media, you will be better off targeting someone who has a following in your niche. A good percentage of the people you follow will get a notification that you have followed them and will take a look at your profile. If they see a professionally presented profile with good quality information they are interested in, they are likely to follow you back.

To manually do this, all you have to do is go to 'my profile' and click on the 'my followers' tab and you will get a long list of each account following me. Just click away at the 'Follow' button on each account and you are now following these people.

The down side to following manually is that it will take you a long time to do, and you will soon enough hit a limit set by Twitter as to how many people you can be following. You are allowed to be following 2,000 people without having anyone following you back. Once you hit 2,000, Twitter then imposes a limit based on how many followers are following you. The ratio limit is not really revealed by Twitter other than they openly advise, regardless of how many people are following you, the maximum daily limit you can follow is 1,000 accounts. As a rule of thumb, you can be following around 10% more accounts than you have following you. So if you had 10,000 followers, you could be following 11,000 accounts.

If you are tweeting great content and you are exposing your Twitter account via your website, in your email signature and any other means available to you, you should be gaining some followers organically.

TWEEPI

Now that you have a professional appearance and are tweeting to a niche on Twitter, you can start the following and unfollowing process that will gain you thousands of highly targeted followers. This is the only program that is web-based, so you do not need to have a windows PC to access it–you can do this from any computer you use daily.

This software is called Tweepi. You will need to set up the Platinum program, which is an annual subscription. The only down side to Tweepi is that each account requires a subscription. You can manage multiple accounts, but you have to pay the annual fee for each account. I suggest you do this first; then, while you have it open on your computer, follow the next steps.

For now just get used to following and unfollowing on a daily basis. Before you even go to Tweepi, open a browser in Chrome. It is best to use Tweepi in the Chrome browser as there is an extension that is only available with Chrome that will save you tons of time.

The easiest way to find this is to do a search on this phrase 'Chrome extension for Tweepi' and then install this on the computer you intend to use for running Tweepi.

Once you have installed the extension, from Chrome go to **www.tweepi.com** and just sign up and log in. Spend some time looking around the options, but for now, on a daily basis you should do the following:

Go down to Premium Unfollow tools and the second tab called 'Unfollow users I followed more than x days ago, and haven't followed me back'. If you have been following people manually, this step will remove anybody that has not followed you back and improve your following-to-follower ratio.

Change the default 30-days setting to five days and hit 'FLUSH THEM'. This will simply bring up a list and show you how many people you are following who are not following you back.

Go to the bottom of the screen and open up the number of images per page to 200; you should only have to do this once. This is where the Chrome extension comes in handy. Instead of unfollowing them one by one, you should see a little yellow icon in the top right-hand corner of your browser that looks like a baby chicken. Note that if you do not see the Tweepi icon, it is likely you have opened Tweepi in a browser other than Chrome.

Click on the Tweepi icon, and it will unfollow everyone on that page. If there are more than 200, go to the bottom and to the next page and do the same—you can do up to a maximum of 1,000, but I suggest at the moment no more than 400 to 600 per day, which is two or three pages each day.

Next go to the 'follow new tweeps' section and the first option you will see is:

'Want to follow new users based on which tweeps they're interested in? Try following an @user's followers'. Type in a user name that you feel is aligned with your niche from the list you have made.

Same as before, have the page open to 200 and then click the Tweepi icon in Chrome; only follow between 400 and 600 people, so again, two or three pages worth. When you are following, make sure the box that says 'Skip previously followed or unfollowed' is highlighted blue.

For now that is all you have to do, and it should take you only five minutes each day. Spend some time to get to know the other features as you go. The one final tip is to keep in mind that Twitter works on a 24-hour time basis as far as daily limits are concerned, so for example do not do your following and unfollowing in the afternoon on one day and then in the morning the next. I suggest you pick a time each day that you will always be able to find five minutes to spare and do it around that time every day.

This is the secret to gaining very targeted followers on Twitter. Once you are proficient in the daily routine, you will grow an exceptional presence your competitors will envy.

CHAPTER 7

Instagram and the secret sauce

Instagram is one of the newer kids on the block in Social Media platforms. It was launched in October 2010, and in April 2012 it was acquired by Facebook for around $1 billion US dollars. To date, it has in excess of 150 million users who have shared almost 16 billion photos. It is here to stay: a recent study concluded that 60% of the world's top brands are now using Instagram. You should be, too.

If you had asked me one year ago in early 2013 if I considered Instagram to have any value as a Social Media option for businesses, my answer would have been very different to now. I recall talking with a couple of our children who were using it at the time and looking at some of the content they were sharing. It was typical teenager stuff: selfies, food, images of friends, etc.

Not having an account of my own, I asked one of them if I could take a look at what other people were posting. After half an hour of surfing through stuff similar to what my children were posting, it seemed like a platform for teenagers to waste some leisure time on, and I was ready to dismiss it as a serious possibility for real marketing.

Over the next couple of months it seemed there were constant mentions of Instagram every time I read blogs or visited groups related to Social Media. It was soon obvious this was not just for the kids and some serious research was warranted. It did not take me too long to see there was some real potential for Instagram; however, it was a platform very different to everything else and would need a very different approach to be useful.

If you have not seriously considered Instagram, don't despair–it is never too late to start. You can have your account up and running in the next 30 minutes. Just follow these simple steps and be open to the incredible opportunities this platform offers.

Whilst you can view your Instagram profile on your computer, you can only set up an account by downloading the app to your smart phone or iPad. Once it has downloaded, create a username and password. Complete your profile information and upload an image and you are done.

Simple enough. However, here are some more in-depth tips to create a great profile and presence.

INSTAGRAM

YOUR PROFILE IMAGE
There is no where other than your profile image that you can add any branding. The main panel above your image and profile information populates with the images you post. You will see they

constantly rotate through your latest posts. The setup process for Instagram for this reason is probably the simplest of any network you will find. It is best to use your company logo as your image for this reason unless you are building a personal following; if this is the case, use your personal head shot image.

ACCOUNT NAME

If possible, use your Twitter handle as your account name or your company name if they are not the same. The more similar all of your Social Media profile names are, the easier you make it for your fans and followers to find you on multiple platforms. It is even more necessary on Instagram as you cannot search by keywords or hashtags for business account names. The work-around for this is to include a hashtag for your account names–#adamhoulahan is mine. You can use up to 30 characters, and it can contain numbers and the underscore. So, if you cannot register exactly the same option as your Twitter handle, use the underscore or numbers to keep as close to it as possible.

YOUR PROFILE

You only have 150 characters, so explain what your business is about as succinctly as possible. There is also an area to add your website URL. Unlike Twitter, the profile supports only one URL, so use your website if that is where you want to drive traffic to.

YOUR IMAGES

Whenever possible, watermark your brand name or website address within the images you post; there is currently no ability like with Pinterest or Tumblr to have anyone viewing your images click on the image and land on your website. The best option is to at least expose your brand within the image. There are many options to enhance images using built-in filters. I don't use the filters as I usually post images I have created for Pinterest as quotes. The filters work best for actual photos you have taken with your phone. If you do post images you have taken on your phone, then by all means have a play around with the filters.

The most popular filters currently are Lo-Fi, which boosts contrast and brings out warm tones; X-Pro II, which has a similar high contrast effect but retains more of the original colour; Amaro, which bleaches photos; Rise, which adds a golden glow and Hudson, which casts a cool light. More than half of all photos still use no filters at all.

HASHTAGS

Adding tags to your photos is essential and is an effective way to reach beyond just your current followers. It is the equivalent of keywords in your blog posts. You can research popular tags to add to your posts. Webstagram features the top 100 tags; start here to see if any of these are appropriate to you **www.web. stagram.com/hot**.

You can also come up with your own unique tags. The more specific your tags are to your niche, the better reach they will get. If you are going to use your own hashtags, make sure your followers are aware of them and encourage them to use them when posting images related to you. Unique tags are essential when you are running photo competitions.

Most platforms work best with just two or three hashtags. Instagram allows you to use up to 30, and I recommend using as many as are relevant to your niche or brand; though realistically, five seems to be a good number without looking too much like spam. Always include your personal hashtag on every image you post as this is the only way someone searching for you can easily find all of your images.

Location tags are very popular as well. You can be a little creative in how you apply your hashtags. Try including some of your hashtags in your description if it is relevant to you–something similar to 'Our top performers recently joined us at our annual #company name #convention in #Hawaii #USA'.

HOW OFTEN SHOULD I POST TO INSTAGRAM?

Post quality not quantity. It is best to post at a much lower rate good quality content. I find one or two posts a day is more than enough, and don't be too concerned if you miss a day or two here and there.

Instagram has been underrated for use by businesses until very recently; most people were of the view it was a platform just for teenagers. Some great strategies are now emerging to promote brands and engagement. You will need to take some time to work out what is the best strategy for your business. Your strategies for each platform you use will vary–how you interact with your followers on Twitter is very different to Pinterest or Google Plus. Instagram is very different from all of these profiles.

A great resource you should spend some time on is Instagram's own blog for businesses; you will find it at **www.business.instagram. com/blog**. Here you will find up-to-date tips on great ways to utilise this photo and now video platform. It regularly gives instances of companies that invent great ways to promote themselves, events or offers, which you can likely copy or use to suit your own needs.

INSTAGRAM STRATEGIES

Depending on the industry your business operates in, there are some key strategies that work well for Instagram.

PHOTO CONTESTS

Photo contests are becoming one of the most popular strategies to use. This simply involves engaging your followers to submit photos through Instagram that are relevant to your business. It may involve them holding a sign with your business name on it to taking 'selfies' at one of your locations or wearing a clothing item you sell or produce. Again there are endless options available; you should plan well ahead and research the 'how-tos' for running photo contests. Google or even the Instagram business blog are your best options to research many companies that are using Photo contests to great effect.

BEHIND THE SCENES LOOK AT YOUR BUSINESS

This is one of my favourites as it is potentially one of the easiest to do. It is a great way to put a human face to your business, with hundreds of options to post every week. You can post images of your team members doing what they do or your production processes in action.

A restaurant might preview images of weekly special dishes, or patrons enjoying a meal (with their permission of course).

If your business is location-based, meaning it is a destination people need to visit to purchase your products or services. Another great option is to register your business location on Foursquare. You can then tag your photos with your location when posting to

Instagram. The app will use foursquare's venue search and feature your business with your photo.

If you have linked your Instagram account to Foursquare, you can also check in when adding photos by clicking on Foursquare in the 'Share' options on your smart phone. The photo will then be added to the public photos displayed at your businesses page on Foursquare.

THE HOW-TO STRATEGY

If you can create a 10 to 15 second quick 'how to' video once a week, you have a great strategy option. Each video may be one step in a process such as 'How to develop a marketing plan in 7 easy steps (Step 1)'. This gives your followers a reason to want to come back to your Instagram profile every week to get the next step. It also allows you to be a little more specific in each video.

They can be any simple quick tip on any subject aligned with your business. If it is valued information, your followers will engage with you regularly and even share your content every week.

The options are endless, and these videos do not need to be exceptionally high-quality productions. If you do not have video production equipment, you can shoot them on your smart phone as long as the lighting is adequate and you speak to a script you have practiced well beforehand. There is plenty of free video editing software available to add your logo, website, etc. Just do a search on the term 'free video editing software' and take your pick.

These are just a handful of strategies you can use, but there are many more. The more you research your strategy options before you launch one, the better your results will be.

GREAT APPS

There is no shortage of apps available to enhance your Instagram experience. Here are eight you should take a look at.

STATIGRAM

Statigram gives you functionality to like and comment on posts or even pin to Pinterest from your computer instead of your smartphone. You can also get statistics on your account, such as the number of new followers you have or who has unfollowed you, the most liked posts and the number of comments you receive.

WEBSTAGRAM

Webstgram is similar to statigram—take a look at them both. Webstagram claim their site is the most popular for viewing photos.

FOLLOWGRAM

Followgram is used by brands such as Ford Motor Company, Ikea, Levi's Armani and more. It enhances the visual experience. Free and annual subscriptions are available.

GRAMFEED

Gramfeed is like a search tool for Instagram. It also allows you to view profiles, pin to Pinterest and like on Facebook.

PHOTOREPOST

As the name suggests, Photorepost allows you to repost images and videos you like to your own photostream. It's great for adding your followers' posts about you to create engagement.

INSTARCHIVE

Instarchive allows you to download all of your photos to a single folder and is great way to back up or reuse across your other networks.

COPYGRAM

Copygram is almost a better option for viewing yours and other accounts on your computer, with options to follow, like and comment. You can also download photos to your computer.

OVERGRAM

One of my personal favourites, this app allows you to take photos on your smart phone and then overlay text to them. You can share directly to Instagram and other profiles from the app, too.

While you work out the best way to utilise Instagram for your company or brand, you should start building your follower base with this very easy daily routine. Like all of the other programs we have covered, this will take only a few minutes each day.

 # THE SECRET SAUCE

The same secret to building a good follower base for Instagram is posting one or two great images per day–quotes are universally loved by all–and following thousands of people who are in your niche. Finding the right people is exactly the same process you followed for Pinterest or Twitter. Find other businesses or people who are in your niche and follow the people that are following them, as they are highly likely to be interested in what you have to offer. Make your list of these accounts because after some months of doing this, it is easy to forget whose followers you have followed before, so keeping track of these is the best way to avoid this.

You can follow these people one by one from your phone (you cannot do it from your computer) if you prefer to and you have plenty of spare time on your hands; however, I prefer to use some software that will take care of this throughout the day for me.

NINJAGRAM

This software is made by the same team that make Ninjapinner for Pinterest, and it works in a very similar manner. To get started, go to **www.ninjagram.com** and download the software to your PC. Once you have done this and gone through the activation process, you should get familiar with all of the setting options available in the tutorials; however, we will cover just the daily following routine. It will be best to have Ninjagram open as we step though this process.

FOLLOWING AND UNFOLLOWING

The first step is to log your Instagram account into Ninjagram. To do this, click the 'Add' tab on the right side of the Ninjagram template. Another box will open over the top of the existing screen with fields to add your username and password. Add these exactly the same as if you were logging into Instagram. Confirm your password and then click continue.

You will now be back at the login screen; click the 'login' tab. You should now be on the menu tab, and the first option is 'gather usernames / photos'. In the middle of the screen, you'll see a section highlighted 'Gather usernames for following or unfollowing'. If this is not highlighted, highlight it now by clicking on the round circle at the front of this tab.

Below this is a drop-down menu with the heading 'gather from'. Open this up and highlight 'User's Followers'. Below this, a new box will appear where you enter the username from your list. Once you have entered this name, click the 'Start gathering IDs' tab.

Ninjagram will now start importing all of the usernames following the account you requested. Once it has finished importing them all, go back to the menu at the top of Ninjagram and select the second option, 'Auto-Follow'. You will see another box where you can enter the number of accounts to follow. Three hundred is considered the most you should follow in a day; I suggest you set it to about 285.

Depending on how long you intend to have your computer running, set your time delay settings in options and then press 'Start Following'. You can now go about your day and Ninjagram will get to work doing your following for you.

The maximum number of accounts you can be following at any given time is 7,500. Once you reach this number or close to it, you will need to unfollow anybody that has not followed you back. Ninjagram will again take care of this for you.

From the main menu, click the third option, which is 'Auto-UnFollow'. Some additional check boxes will now appear. Tick the check boxes you wish to activate and click the 'start unfollowing' tab. You can again go about your day and leave Ninjagram to do the work for you.

As you will see, Ninjagram has more features than just this follow and unfollow process. Take your time to see if its other features suit your purposes. Once you are used to the software and how it works, this process should only take you five minutes each day to set and forget.

CHAPTER 8

Tumblr and the secret sauce

Tumblr made its debut in February 2007, and while it is still one of the lesser-known platforms for business purposes, here are some statistics that may convince you to take a look.

There are currently more than 160 million blogs registered, with 125,000 new registrations per day. These blogs have now uploaded more than 70 billion blog posts. The daily average number of posts is now more than 95 million. Page views are in excess of five billion every month. In 2013, Yahoo purchased Tumblr for more than $1 billion in cash. It is a serious Social Media platform with more than 200 staff to keep it running.

Currently, Tumblr's largest audience is 18 to 30 years old, but if your target market is not in this age group, it does not mean you should not be building a follower base. Some of the world's best known brands are using Tumblr to great effect–brands like Coca-Cola, Nabisco, Calvin Klein, Lexus, Ford Motor Company, Sesame Street and many more.

WHAT IS TUMBLR?

Tumblr is essentially a micro-blogging platform. It supports text, photos, links, chat, audio and video. If you have attempted to create a stand-alone blog before, you are well aware of the time and energy that goes into its creation and maintenance and the huge hurdle of getting followers to your content. Tumblr overcomes all of these issues. You can set up a blog in minutes, it is very user friendly to upload multiple types of content and it's very easy to build a follower base. One of the most useful features I like is the way hashtags are created: simply start typing a word in the tag section and a number of related tags are featured for you to consider using.

The huge popularity Tumblr enjoys comes down to the flexibility to customise, the ease of uploading content, and the incorporation of social tools such as the ability to 'like' comments on posts and share or 'reblog', as it is known.

SETTING UP YOUR ACCOUNT

There are endless themes both free and paid to allow you to customise the look and feel of your blog to suit your business or personal image. Many themes also allow you to incorporate Google Analytics so you can track the engagement you create. I would highly recommend choosing a theme that does support Analytics for this very reason.

Unlike setting up a Blogger or WordPress blog, getting started on Tumblr is quite easy. I suggest you spend a little time before you set up your account and have a look around at what other businesses and brands are using it to great effect. There are hundreds of themes to choose from; find one that is aligned with your current website or branding.

Once you have decided on a theme (don't worry, you can change themes at anytime), it is time to start setting up your account. Go to the Tumblr home page at **www.tumblr.com**. You will need to supply an email address, password and the URL of your blog. You will notice Tumblr will add '.tumblr.com' to the end of the URL, so essentially you are customising the first half of the URL–hopefully with your business or brand name. It is possible your first choice will not be available, so have a few options you are happy with ready to try. Keep it as short and memorable as possible. Note also that it is possible to have a customised URL if you cannot find anything that suits you. It does require a little extra work in the set up process, and you can find some basic information here: **http:// www.tumblr.com/docs/en/custom_domains** This is an area you may want to get some expert assistance with if you decide to use a custom domain.

You will need to verify your account, so make sure you have easy access to the email account you supplied. Once you have verified your account, you can start adding your theme and customising colours, fonts, etc. Depending on the theme you choose, this process will vary; however, it is generally straight forward enough. If colour and design is not something you excel at, you may want to use Fiverr.com or Elance.com or, if you already have a website designer or graphic artist, get them involved at this point. Waiting for them to finalise these small but important features should not stop you from getting started with your blogging.

Everyone is going mobile these days. Ensure you incorporate a mobile version within your design to accommodate the thousands of people viewing your content on smart phones and tablets. If the theme you have chosen does not have a mobile version, choose another theme. It is usually as simple as activating the mobile tab in the advanced options; you should not need to have any technical IT skills to have this option on Tumblr.

There are plenty of tutorials on setting up your account. Just do a search on the phrase 'setting up a Tumblr blog' and you will have plenty of YouTube videos or basic tutorials to choose from to assist you. Tumblr has a very detailed help centre you can utilise as well. Once you have everything set up to your liking, it is time to start blogging.

STRATEGIES

Tumblr is all about images, animated gifs, videos and quotes. You can be a little more creative than with a standard blog, and you will find your followers will be a lot more interactive on Tumblr than followers to your WordPress or other blog platforms. The key is to create content that your followers will like to comment on and share. It needs to be fresh, enticing and always very visually appealing.

If you can solve problems, tell stories, make people laugh and inspire them, you have the basis for a good content strategy. The best part if you are using Instagram—you probably already have everything you need.

QUOTES

Quotes are always a great place to start. As you are already creating some great image-based quotes for your other networks, simply use the same content here on Tumblr. One good quote per day should be enough.

A BEHIND-THE-SCENES LOOK AT YOUR BUSINESS

This is one of my favourites as it is potentially one of the easiest to do. It is a great way to put a human face to your business, with hundreds of options to post every week. You can post images of your team members doing what they do, or your production processes in action.

A ladies clothing store might show images of the latest designs that have arrived or accessories that would be a good match to a particular dress.

Your followers always love to know what is going on in your world—just like the Instagram strategy of showing behind-the-scenes images of your team doing what they do or having fun throughout their day. Short videos or images you have created for Instagram again will be fine; recycle that great content here, too.

Your Instagram strategy of creating how-to videos can also be recycled here on Tumblr, which makes Tumblr a good fit with Instagram as a strategy. The options are endless, and these videos do not need to be exceptionally high-quality productions.

Again, in sharing any simple, quick tip on any subject aligned with your business, if it is valued information, your followers will engage with you regularly and even share your content every week.

CAUSES

Does your business support any causes, charities or local events? If so, tell the world through Tumblr. Apart from giving these great operations a much needed free promotion once or twice per week, you have some great content to share. Your followers and customers/clients will always view any support you give with a high degree of respect.

It is highly likely these organisations will already do the hard work for you in content creation; you can simply share the images or links they produce on your profile. A simple message asking to re-share the content or letting your followers know what you did to support them recently is all you need to add.

Cause-related marketing has many benefits to any business, including increased sales, customer loyalty, improved corporate image and often valuable media coverage. If your business is not supporting any of these organisations, you are missing an important opportunity. This does not have to be a huge financial burden–any support you can give will be greatly appreciated. One simple option is to support your team members by offering them a paid day off every six months to assist an organisation by donating their time. Or simply contact an organisation you feel personally aligned with and ask them how you can help.

GREAT OFFERS OR PROMOTIONS

A word of caution! Use this option sparingly. Save it for your best offers, and never use it for more than 5% of your total Social Media content. Consider creating an offer that is exclusive to your followers on Tumblr. Using a promotion or redemption code that is revealed only on the site is a good way to track the success of these campaigns.

Another good option to create engagement is to reward your followers for sharing your content. It could be as simple as thanking them publicly online or giving them a free 'something'. If they feel appreciated and heard by your business, they will quickly move from just followers to brand advocates.

HASHTAGS

Tumblr loves hashtags, so much so that it has its own section to add them to each post to make it as easy as possible to add them. There does not seem to be a limit on how many tags you can add per post; however, as a rule of thumb, more than five looks spammy.

Unlike other platforms, Tumblr does allow you to have multiple word tags, such as 'Famous Quotes'. On any other platform, you would need to use 'FamousQuotes' as one word. When searching tags on Tumblr, ensure you type them as two words, not one. Or just click directly onto a tag you like to see similar posts using the same tag.

There is no need to use content hashtags, simply add your tags after each post in the section provided. Ensure you add your branded tags each time.

GREAT APPS AND EXTENSIONS

There are some great apps available to enhance your use of Tumblr. Here are six you should take a look at.

TUMBLR BOOKMARKLET

This is Tumblr's own app, and it is available from **http://www.tumblr.com/apps**. It allows you to share any content you find directly to your blog. You will also find mobile versions for IOS, Windows and Android phones.

TUMBLRSTATS

This gives you comprehensive statistics about your Tumblr profile. There is no requirement to create an account: just add your Tumblr name, and Tumblrstats will create a nice graph with details on the number of posts, frequency and type of posts, time since last post, etc. It is worth taking five minutes once per month to log into.

POSTLING

Postling is not a free service, but for most users, the $10 per month plan should suffice. It has many features beyond just Tumblr. The editor has more formatting options than the standard Tumblr editor, so it's well worth taking a look.

ZEMANTA

This is only available using the Firefox, Internet Explorer, Chrome, or Safari browsers. It enhances Tumblr's editor.

Zemanta improves your regular blogging dashboard. It recommends **images, links, articles and tags** while you write. It allows you to enrich your own content and link to other media with as little effort as possible–a single click. With Zemanta you can easily:

- insert images into your blog post
- insert links to related articles (from 300,000 newsfeeds and blogs)
- link back to your own blog posts
- add affiliate links

TUMBLRHELPER

This adds a number of useful features to Tumblr; however, it is only available in the Chrome browser.

Regarding new post templates, you can save common settings (tags, always add to queue, fields, etc.) to set as default for new posts. These are specific to a given post type (photo, quote, etc.) and you can add signatures, post formatting templates, etc.

Add personal notes about users on your dashboard, such as 'Why did I start following this person?' or 'This person always compliments my posts'.

- Delete button on edit post pages.
- Page reloading
- Delete posts via nice little ajax loader.
- Open links in new windows on the dashboard and similar pages when endless scrolling is enabled.
- Go back to new posts page after posting (instead of dashboard).

TUMBLRPOST

This is only available for Firefox. It lets you post photos, videos, MP3s, quotes and links to your Tumblr tumblelogs by dragging and dropping content on to the extension's status bar icon or through the 'Post to my tumblelog' menu items in the content's context menu. There is no need to save images, files, etc. to your hard drive. Just post directly to Tumblr.

 THE SECRET SAUCE

The secret to building a good follower base for Tumblr is really no different to most other platforms. Post a few great images each day, and since quotes are universally loved by all people on all platforms, use them here, too. Follow thousands of people who are in your niche, and a good percentage always follows you back. Finding the right people is exactly the same process you follow for Pinterest or Twitter. Find other businesses or people who are in your niche and follow the people that are following them. Make your list of these accounts, and keep a record of who you have followed. After a few months of doing this, it is easy to forget whose followers you have followed before.

TUMBLENINJA

This software is made by the same team that make Ninjapinner for Pinterest, and it works in a very similar manner. To get started, go to **ninjapinner.com/tumbleninja-tumblr-bot/** and download the software to your PC. Once you have done this and have gone through the activation process, you should get familiar with all of the setting options available in the tutorials; however, we will cover the daily routine to follow. It will be best to have TumbleNinja open as we step though this process.

FOLLOWING AND UNFOLLOWING

The first step is to log your Tumblr account into TumbleNinja. To do this, click the 'Add' tab on the right side of the template. Another box will open over the top of the existing screen with fields to add your email and password. Add these exactly the same as if you were logging into your Tumblr account. Confirm your password and then click 'continue'. Note you must use the email address that is attached to your Tumblr account, not your username.

You will now be back at the login screen; click the 'login' tab. You should now be on the menu tab, and the first option is 'Auto-Follow'. At the bottom half of the screen, you will see a drop-down menu headed 'Target'. The options you can use to find people to follow are Tag Search, Blog Search, Post Notes and Google Search. Experiment with them all to find what best suits your business.

Beside the Target menu to the right is a section to add your search term; simply add the term you want to search here. Under this tab is a section to put the number of people you wish to follow. I suggest you keep this to around 285 per 24 hours. Then, below this is a 'Start Following' tab; once you are ready, click this tab.

TumbleNinja will now start importing all of the usernames you requested. Once it has finished importing them, it will automatically commence following.

Depending how long you intend to have your computer running, set your time delay settings in options along with any other setting options you choose. You can now go about your day, and TumbleNinja will get to work doing your following for you.

The maximum number of accounts you can be following at any given time is 5,000. Once you reach this number or close to it, you will need to unfollow anybody that has not followed you back. TumbleNinja will again take care of this for you.

From the main menu, click the second option: 'Auto-UnFollow'. Some additional check boxes will now appear. Tick the check boxes you wish to activate and click the 'start unfollowing' tab. You can again go about your day and leave Ninjagram to do the work for you.

As you will see, TumbleNinja has more features than just this follow and unfollow process. Take your time to see if its other features suit your purposes. Once you are used to the software and how it works, this process should take you only five minutes each day to set and forget.

CHAPTER 9

Google Plus and the secret sauce

WHAT IS GOOGLE PLUS?

Yes, it is another Social Media platform similar to Twitter, Pinterest, Facebook, Tumblr and Instagram. So why do we need yet another platform to manage? As we have covered earlier, there are so many Social Media options, it is impossible to be active on them all. Yet Google Plus simply must be one you choose to build a following on.

It can be a little overwhelming for the first-time user. There are multiple options, from a personal profile to pages and communities. I will cover some basics here to help you get started. Keep in mind that this book is predominantly about growing your follower bases. So if you have never used Google Plus before, it may be worth doing some more in-depth research on the basics we cover before you create your account.

It does have two compelling reasons why you should be using it now:

1. Because it is owned by Google! Google is the king of search engines, with more than 65% of all searches performed on the platform every day. When you link and verify your website to your Google Plus account, sharing content on your Google Plus account is ranked highly by Google as good quality content. This will improve your visibility in searches and lead more clients or customers to you over time.

2. Google continues to create high quality features that integrate well together, such as Gmail; Google Drive, Calendar, Maps, YouTube and more. No doubt these will build over the coming years into a well-designed platform packed with features and functionality.

There are many opinions on the true number of current users of Google Plus; they range from 550 million down to 300 million depending on how you wish to measure use of the platform. However, it is almost universally accepted that the numbers are growing at an incredible rate given it has only been in existence since 2011, and all businesses should be building their presence here as soon as possible.

SETTING UP A GOOGLE PLUS ACCOUNT

Assuming you have not already registered a Google Plus profile, follow this step-by-step guide to setting yours up now.

1. Go to **https://plus.google.com**. You will be directed to a page to input your details to create your account. By default, whether you want one or not, you will be required to set up a Gmail

email account. You will still be able to log in using other email accounts; however, choose an email address you will want to keep; once you get used to Google's many features, you are highly likely to use this often. After you have input your name, password, etc., you will need to verify the account via an email link sent to your current email account.

2. Add a photo you are happy to have visible on the account. It will appear in a round circle shape, so generally just a head shot works best.

3. At this point, your account is set up in a basic form; however, you will be walked through finding friends to connect with and interesting people and pages (in Google's opinion). These are optional steps you can choose to do or skip. After this process, you will be able to add employment details, schools you attended, and where you live–again, all optional information.

4. You will now enter an optional welcome to the Google Plus tour, which will only take a few minutes (however, it is again optional). In the top left corner is a drop-down menu defaulted to 'Home'. Click on this and go to the second menu option, 'profile'. This is what anyone navigating directly to your profile would see, so ensure you are happy with what is visible. You can add a nicer profile background by choosing from the supplied gallery or by uploading an image of your own. The latter is the best option as far as promoting what you are about.

In the 'about' section, fill out as much detail as possible in as many sections as possible. Ensure you add links to every other profile you have. Let people searching your profile have a very clear understanding of what you are about.

You have now set up your personal profile on Google Plus, but you will also need a page. To create a page, you must first have a personal profile. You can have as many pages as you choose attached to your profile. These next steps are for setting up a page.

5. In the top right corner, you will see your profile image–click on this. A pop-up screen will appear; click the 'create a page' tab. You will need to choose what type of page your will set up; choose the one most appropriate to you. Depending on which option you choose, the setup process will vary slightly; however, it is an easy step-by-step process similar to setting up your profile.

Once you have completed the steps, you are set with both your personal profile and page. So what is the difference between a profile, a page and a community?

PERSONAL PROFILE VS. PAGES AND COMMUNITIES

To explain this in simple terms, think of a profile as being about you and a page as being about your business. A community could be a group of like-minded people who share a common passion such as organic gardening, horses, etc. Your business may be a member of multiple communities on Google Plus or you may start one of your own.

Whilst they look very similar, there are some key points of difference between a profile and a page that may explain why you need to have both:

You are the only person who can control your page (unless you give your password access to another person). A page can have multiple people accessing the account. These are called Managers or Communication Managers.

Pages have more options to customise, and you can add a specific location. Your profile can only be as specific as a town or city in any given country.

Unlike most other platforms, Google Plus allows you to sort followers in a way that is meaningful to you. It allows you to have multiple 'circles', and you can add people to different circles for different reasons. For example, if you have offices in multiple countries and want to post something that is only relative to, say, your Australian office, you can choose to post it only to the people in your 'Australia' circle. A page can only post to its own circles and communities; you can post to extended circles and groups from your profile.

Here are some great apps and tools you might like to take a look at to enhance your value on Google Plus.

APPS AND TOOLS

RIPPLES

Every post you or anyone else makes has the 'ripples' feature. To access it, go to the drop-down menu on the post itself in the top right corner. At the very bottom will be a tab, 'view ripples'. Click on this and the post's ripples will appear. You can view the ripples of any post, not just your own. Go and take a look at one now–just find a post by anyone that is showing a lot of re-shares and click on its 'view ripples' tab. What you are now seeing are the details of every person who publicly shared the post. If you hover over their name, a pop-up will appear allowing you to view the post on their profile or 'follow' their account.

You may also see a ripple within a ripple. This feature is showing the people who shared the post and then the post was re-shared from their account. This helps you to start to identify who the influential people are within any field of expertise. A list of the most influential people will also be visible at the very bottom the ripple page, on the left under the heading 'Influencers'. On the far right of the page will be a list of every person who has shared the post, a link to their profile and the post they shared onto their account. This is a very handy feature when you have posts with a large volume of shares.

Take some time to get used to how ripples work and the data they are making available to you. We will be covering ripples in more detail within the strategy section of this chapter very soon.

AUTHORSHIP

Now that you have your account set up, you should activate the authorship feature. To do this, just go to plus.google.com/authorship and sign up with your email address. A verification link will be sent; click on this and follow the steps. It should be a simple process you can complete yourself without too much IT assistance, if any.

This is the easy part; it does get a little trickier when you post content. Some simple steps that will make it much easier are to ensure that you have a photo of yourself on your Google Plus account, that you have an email address on the same domain as your blog and that your byline on your blog is on every page of content and is the same as your Google Plus byline. I suggest from here you follow the instructions on the Google Authorship page.

The value of Google Authorship lies in the verification of content you find on the web and the connection to the creator of the content. You can distinguish verified content by the Google Plus image of the author and the number of circles the author is showing under the link when you do a search. If you are the author, then the value is huge from the point of influence, visibility and clicks on your links to your blog, etc.

Potentially, in the medium term, authorship could dramatically reduce spam as people doing searches become accustomed to the link between the verified content and non-verified content.

REPLIES AND MORE

Replies and More is a chrome extension for Google Plus. It primary feature is adding the ability to reply directly to the author or anyone in the conversation thread with a single click. Without Replies and More it is still possible to manually do this by typing the persons name and adding the '+' symbol in front of their name. So essentially, this is a big time-saving tool.

It also adds the ability to share the post directly to Facebook and Twitter or to email a link to anyone. Without the extension you can only re-share on Google Plus. A couple of additional features you can turn on if you choose are a desktop notification and chime; these are not set as defaults, so you will need to go into the settings to activate these.

HANGOUT MAGIX

Hangout Magix allows you to add your own banners across a video image while you are on a hangout. This allows you to display your contact details, calls to action or promote links to other Social Media platforms. If you are doing hangouts or plan to in the future, this tool is worth taking a look at.

CIRCLECOUNT

Now that you have your Google Plus profile set up, you should register your account in CircleCount. It is very easy to do and free. Just go to **www.circlecount.com** to register. CircleCount keeps track of your followers and following history, comments, +1s and shares on your posts. It will also benchmark your profile by all profiles registered in the world and split this by gender. You will also see your rank for the country you have your profile registered in, again split by gender.

Apart from data on your own account information, you can view profiles, pages or communities of other people or companies in categories such as most followed or most popular. There are some handy statistics and the ability to compare profiles against each other or brands against each other, such as Pepsi vs. Coca Cola. Once you have registered, have a look around CircleCount to familiarise yourself with all of the available data.

The Chrome browser again has a great extension you can download free which gives you very interesting information about users directly to your browser.

How you use this information will depend on whether you are a brand, small business or just as an individual. It will allow you to compare the engagement of different types of posts such as quotes, funny images, etc. This is very helpful information as you compare different content strategy results into the future. You can also search for people who are likely to be interested in 'what you do' by searching on tags like 'health and fitness' or 'food bloggers'. We will cover this more in the section 'Gaining followers'.

You can view how many people you have in circles directly from Google Plus; however, if you want to easily track new circles you have been added to or to thank these people for adding you, Circle Count makes this much easier.

RECOMMENDEDUSERS.COM

This is another useful website to assist you in finding good people to add to your circles. This site is not owned or endorsed by Google Plus. There are multiple categories to choose from plus featured users. Featured users are paying to be listed in the side bar of each page, and whilst they may have great profiles or interesting content, they may not technically be high profile or highly followed. Being a featured user is a great way to get your account exposed to tens of thousands of people very quickly. As always, if you are going to pay to be featured on sites like these, you will need to have great content first if you hope to attract new followers.

CIRCLOSCOPE

Circlescope is another Chrome extension. It is not a free tool; however, it does have a trial version you can try first. The maximum number of people you can follow is limited to 5,000 currently on Google Plus. This is a great tool for tracking your followers and people you are following. It is packed with great features to help you effectively manage your circles.

Use the filter options to group people with similar interests into their own circles. You can filter by locations, professions or interests, such as Social Media, bloggers, musicians or almost anything you find useful.

One of its most powerful tools is the ability to filter by how often the people you are following have had any interaction on Google Plus. You can set the time limits to whatever you choose: days, weeks, months and then collate all of these people together. You have the option to create either a new circle for them to see if they increase their interactions or unfollow all of them in one click.

If you are close to the 5,000 follow limit, this can be a simple way to evaluate who you should continue to follow and who it may be worth dropping to allow you to follow more engaged people. Alternatively, you may wish to make a list of all of the people you have followed who have not followed you back. These people would again be good candidates for you to unfollow if you are getting close to your 5,000 follow limit.

You may also choose to find and add people who are highly engaged on a post you find interesting. All of these options and many more are available through Circloscope's premium service–it is well worth the small purchase price.

FRIENDS+ME

This is one of my favourite tools; I use it all the time. Again, there is a free version and a paid version. The paid version obviously gives you a much higher degree of functionality. Start with the free option until you fully understand it and then upgrade to the paid version.

Essentially, Friends+Me allows you to spread your Google Plus content across multiple networks with links right back to your Google Plus post. You can spread your Google Plus posts to other Google Plus profiles and pages; Facebook profiles, groups and pages; Twitter; LinkedIn profiles, groups and pages and to Tumblr.

The functionality is excellent, with options to choose how many and at what times you post to each network independently of each other. So, for example, you may wish to post only twice a day to Twitter–once in the morning and once in the evening–yet have four posts to Tumblr at completely separate times. Through the use of tags you can also separate content for each network. This allows you to have different Google Plus content going to each network independent of each other in a more targeted way rather than just the time and number of posts per network options.

Using multiple networks tools like Friends+Me allows you be very time efficient. These tools are crucial in keeping your time commitments to one hour per day.

GAINING FOLLOWERS

So hopefully by now you have set up your Google Plus profile and page, you have checked out some of these great tools and you've become familiar with posting and navigating around these amazing platforms. It is time to start building your followers.

The bad news is at this point in time there are no programs like Ninjapinner or Tweepi that make this a simple process. You are going to have to put some effort into building your follower base. The good news is this does not have to be a difficult or highly time-consuming process if you follow the process I am about to outline for you.

SHARED CIRCLES

Getting invited to the right circles is the fastest and most effective way to grow your follower base and at the same time align yourself with people in your niche or industry. Once you find shared circles filled with your type of people, the key is to interact with these people. Google Plus is all about interaction. If you have just started out on your Google Plus journey, then you are in a great position to commence using shared circles. If you have been using Google Plus for some time and are following lots of people and they are not following you back, now would be a good time to get Circloscope and clean up those circles to give yourself some room to follow some real engagers (remember your 5,000 follower limit–there are no exceptions). Start by commenting on posts, sharing great posts and giving +1s to as many posts and comments as are relevant to you. This shows the people in these circles that you are worth following, and they are also likely to engage in a similar manner with your posts.

The best way to find these special circles is to use the shared circles data base in CircleCount. At **www.circlecount.com/ sharedcircles** and **www.publiccircles.appspot.com** you will find thousands of shared circles listed. You can also use these sites to find any public shared circles you have already been added to.

Another good option is to search Google Plus using hashtags such as: #sharedcircles, #followfriday, #followfridaycircle, #circleoftheday, #circleshare, #circlesharing, #publiccirclesproject and #circleoftheday. There are plenty more of these, but this should give you the idea.

Usually, these circles will have specific instructions on how you can be added to the circles. Generally, this will involve you adding the entire circle to your profile, giving a +1 to the post regarding the circle and sharing the post regarding the circle. These will generally be updated each week or so. Once you get added to the circle, most of the existing members will add you in the next circle share and all new members will need to add you. Through these circle shares, you could be adding up to 500 new people in each share, so you can see how you can reach your 5,000 maximum follows very quickly. Take the time to find the best circles in your niche and use Circloscope to ensure you keep only the most active people long term. You will quickly build thousands of engaged followers with this one simple routine.

Once you have a few thousand followers and fully understand circle shares and how to use Circloscope, you can move to the next level of circle sharing and start creating your own circle shares. The beauty of creating your own circle shares is you are in full control of who is added to the circles. You can build circles of very targeted people within your niche very quickly. You will also be viewed as somewhat of an expert in your field on Google Plus.

I would not recommend attempting this until you have mastered your entire Social Media program across all of the networks you choose to use. It is a very powerful way to build your presence on Google Plus, but it is not for beginners. Running your own public circle shares will take some extra research and commitment to your weekly routines. Be careful not to attempt too much too soon.

GOOGLE COMMUNITIES

Communities on Google Plus are similar to groups on LinkedIn or Facebook; they tend to be very specific to a niche or industry. Some you can just join at will and some are restricted and will require an invite from the creator or managers of the community.

To find Communities, go to the drop-down menu in the top left corner of your page or profile and click on the green communities icon. Here you can see all community invitations you have received; the longer you have been active on Google Plus, the more invites you will get. If you find you have been invited to a community that is likely to be of interest of you, just click on the image for it and click the 'accept invite' button in the top right corner. The same as with any profile or page you are following, you will now see posts by the community in your feed each day.

Below the invitations section is a list of communities you have joined. This is the best way to view and interact with your communities. I would suggest joining only communities you have a real interest in. Communities on Google are similar to real life–you will get out of them what you put in. So you will want to visit and engage with your communities regularly. If you have just started your Google Plus journey, the next section is likely the one you need to concentrate on.

This section is called Discover Communities and is where you can search for communities to join. Google will recommend some for you; however, you can also search for any topic at the top right corner or bottom of the page. For example, type in 'Circle shares' and you will find plenty of communities dedicated to this with hundreds of thousands of members.

Take a little time to search through all of the communities in your niche and then join the ones that look the most interesting or engaged. The more you post, +1 and interact within these communities, the more your follower numbers will increase.

Once you have been around some communities for a while, you could try starting your own. They are very easy to set up: you will see the blue 'create community' tab next to the search at the top of the communities page. Just click on this and follow the step-by-step process. Just like circle shares, this is not for beginners. You need to have spent some time getting familiar with Google Plus and have been actively participating in some communities before you go down this path. You will also need to allocate additional time every week to manage your community or collaborate with some people you trust to manage your community with you.

YOUR WEBSITE

You should add a 'Following on Google Plus' badge to your website linking to your page. All of the main platforms like WordPress or Joomla will have simple plug-ins for this. Anyone visiting your website can then follow you on Google Plus with a simple click of the mouse without even being on Google Plus at the time.

This also assists your website's SEO ranking. The current and even greater future importance Google Plus will have in terms of SEO suggests you should ensure you also have Social Media share buttons for your content on every page, if possible. These are again very simple plug-ins that can be added to your site in minutes. Ask your IT people for some assistance if you can't do this by yourself.

There are other ways to build your follower numbers on Google Plus; however, I have found circle, shares and communities the best options to do this in a time-efficient manner. Here is my daily strategy recommendation to get you started.

STRATEGY

You should be very familiar with HootSuite and scheduling posts by now. So hopefully you are creating content to use across all of your networks and sharing at least two or three per day on Google Plus. It is critical that you do this almost daily or at least as often as you possibly can. Similar to Pinterest, you also need to share other people's content, comment on their posts and give +1s to appropriate content and people.

 ## THE SECRET SAUCE

To build a great following on Google Plus, you will need to add the following daily routines to your schedule on top of posting some of your own content via HootSuite. This should take you no more than 15 minutes per day.

1) Spend five minutes searching for circle shares or communities that are aligned with your business or niche. Follow the instructions on the circle shares to be added to the next share, and comment in the

comments section including the creator of the circle's name. Make sure you add the '+' symbol in front of their name to ensure they are notified of your comment. The +1 comments from other people on your posts are the equivalent to "liking" a comment on Facebook. You should receive notifications to your email each time a new circle share takes place, so check the email you have attached to your Google Plus account for these notifications.

2) +1 20 to 30 posts from your followers or people you are following. To do this, just scroll through your feed–any posts showing here are from the people you follow. Try to ensure you +1 posts from a variety of people, not just the same person each time.

3) Comment on five posts with same process as adding +1s as outlined in Daily tasks #2. Just scroll through your feed and leave a positive comment under any posts you find useful.

4) Share two posts to your profile. A great option is to share the posts you have commented on above in #3. The last three steps are about being social and supporting your community. If you are seen to be active and sharing, commenting, etc., people are more likely to follow you or follow back.

Make sure you schedule your own posts an hour or two after you do this. You do not want all of your posts to happen at the same time. If you have a time allocated each day to your Social Media activities, it should make this a lot easier to manage. If you are using HootSuite effectively, it is likely you have scheduled a number of posts across multiple days in advance. Keep your schedule in mind when you are doing this and schedule your posts for later in the day.

So that is it. Follow these steps and you will be a master of Google Plus in no time at all. I truly believe this is potentially the most important network you can build for the future of your business or brand. I have really only skimmed the surface of Google Plus and its many features and options to give you an understanding of building your follower base.

If you have spare time, research everything you can find on Google Plus and become familiar with all it has to offer. Once you have worked your way through all of its features, you will see it has so much more to offer and how it will become the most important tool in your Social Media strategy.

Conclusion

In this book, I have shared my best knowledge and experience to show you how to build followers in just one hour a day. I use all of these platforms and have shown you how I built these networks to a combined total of over 200,000 followers. I am not suggesting you should use every one of these platforms; I would advise as a business or brand you choose up to three that are highly likely to resonate with your customers or clients and focus on them.

The strategies outlined are designed to build your presence, reputation and followers and should be viewed as a starting point in your Social Media marketing campaign. Every business or brand is different, and many will implement these strategies at a different pace. If you are looking for instant results, this is not the program for you. It is no different to building trust and reputation in yourself or your business. Time, dedication and a professional approach is essential to success. It is the building phase that will give you the momentum and presence in the Social Media world to then implement a more targeted marketing strategy–and with much less reliance on the very expensive low ROI campaigns you may have been using or considering until now.

Once you have done your research and planning, have standardised your branding across all platforms and have perfected your website, you should be able to achieve your desired results if you diligently commit one hour each day over a 12-month period. Like most things in life, you will get out what you put in.

The Social Media landscape is a fast-paced and evolving juggernaut, yet the simple actions of providing high-quality content at a slow but constant daily pace has stood the test of time. If your customers or clients feel they are getting massive value from your content, you are well on your way to creating an army of brand ambassadors who will sing your praises and share your content far and wide.

Please connect with me on any of my profiles. You will find them all on my website at **www.adamhoulahan.com**.

By now you would be well aware that I love quotes. I want to leave you with one of my favourites:

'It is not enough that we do our best; sometimes we must do what is required'.–Sir Winston Churchill.

Lightning Source UK Ltd.
Milton Keynes UK
UKOW07f2342010215

245460UK00012B/253/P